Hello

CROCHET!

You'll be hooked in no time

PAVILION

First published in the United Kingdom in 2014 by
Pavilion Books Company Limited
1 Gower Street
London
WC1E 6HD

ISBN 978-1-91023-105-0

A CIP catalogue record for this book is available
from the British Library.

10 9 8 7 6 5 4 3 2 1
W
Reproduction by Mission, Hong Kong
Printed and bound by 1010 Printing International Ltd, China

This book can be ordered direct from the publisher at
www.pavilionbooks.com

Contents

The Basics

Hooks and yarns

Although you only need a hook and a ball of yarn in order to start crocheting, some hooks will suit you better than others, and some yarns will suit a particular project better than others, too.

Hooks

These are available in a variety of shapes and materials, ranging from aluminium through to expensive hardwoods. The important thing is to find a type that you find comfortable to work with. Some are fitted with a 'grip' or an easy-to-hold handle that can help speed up your work.

In this book, crochet hook sizes are shown for both the European and American market. In Europe, sizes are given metrically (for example, 4.00mm), whereas the US uses its own unique system in which sizes are described by a letter and a number (for example, the US equivalent of a 4.00mm hook is G-6). You may also find that some yarns work better with certain types of hooks; try to build up a good selection so that you are always prepared.

Yarns

There is no end to the range of yarns and fibres that you can crochet with, from fine mohair and lace-weight yarns through to chunky and ribbon yarns. If you are fairly new to the craft, it is probably best to stick to a good-quality cotton or a wool and cotton mix. The advantage of using cotton is that it is easier to 'read' the stitches you have worked.

Once you have selected your yarn, you will want to know what size hook to use. This information can be found on the ball band of the yarn and is usually supplied in terms of knitting needle size. The same size will usually apply to the crochet hook that you need to use. However, if you find your crochet work comes out too tight, try moving up a hook size; if it seems too loose, move down a size.

Metric/European crochet hook sizes	US crochet hook sizes
2.25mm	B-1
2.50mm	–
2.75mm	C-2
3.00mm	–
3.25mm	D-3
3.50mm	E-4
3.75mm	F-5
4.00mm	G-6
4.50mm	7
5.00mm	H-8
5.50mm	I-9
6.00mm	J-10
6.50mm	K-10½
7.00mm	–
8.00mm	L-11
9.00mm	M/N-13
10.00mm	N/P-15

NB: there are not always equivalent sizes in both systems; if you cannot obtain the size of hook suggested in the pattern, use the closest size available. Make a tension/gauge swatch before you start a project in case you need to size up or down.

When selecting yarn, always consider whether it is suitable for the project you have in mind; for example, will it wear well? Does the colour work?

You should also make sure that you have sufficient yarn in matching dye lots to complete your project, as even a slight difference in colours between dye lots can show up quite markedly. Make sure that you are happy with and understand the washing instructions. Ultimately, you want to enjoy your project, so choose a yarn that you find pleasing to work with in terms of texture, composition and colour.

Other useful items

You will probably own many of these items already, but it is useful to collect the following together to help you with your crochet projects.

Scissors

Make sure that these are sharp and used only for cutting yarn.

Tape measure

You will need this for checking your tension (gauge) and for working to specific measurements within a project.

Stitch markers

These items are useful for marking your position when working in the round or for identifying pattern repeats. They are also helpful when joining long seams together.

Pins

You will need long rustproof pins when pinning out work ready for blocking or for joining seams together. I find pins with coloured heads work best, as they stand out from the crochet work.

Sewing-up needle

You will find that seams can be crocheted together in many projects, but a blunt-ended needle will be useful when you need to sew up a seam or weave in any loose ends that cannot be crocheted in.

Sketchbook

This is a useful place to keep ideas, pages from magazines and sources of inspiration. A ring-bound notebook is usually a good option so that you can store swatches, yarn wraps and information relating to hook size and tension.

Project bag

Not only will this stop you losing things, but it will keep your work clean and tidy too. The only problems may occur when you have several projects on the go at the same time!

The crochet stitches

Crochet is a wonderfully versatile craft; knowing just a small number of basic stitches allows you to make a huge range of crocheted objects, homewares and accessories. In this section, we outline the techniques for making some of the most commonly used stitches.

NB: in this book, we use UK crochet terms and names for stitches first, with the US equivalents given in brackets. This can sometimes appear confusing, as the same abbreviation can be used to refer to two different stitches in the two systems. A full list of the abbreviations used in this book, together with a list of UK/US translations, is given on p. 46–47.

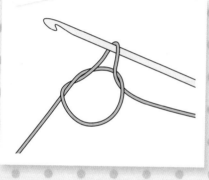

Slipknot

To start a piece of crochet, you will first need to make a loop of yarn to place on the hook, and secure it with a slipknot (1). Leaving a tail end of about 10cm (4in), make a loop in the yarn by wrapping it once around the fingers of your left hand. Pass the tip of the crochet hook through the loop and over the ball end of the yarn with the hook facing down. Use the hook to catch the ball end of the yarn and pull it back through the loop. Pull gently on the tail end of the yarn to tighten the slipknot around the hook.

Chain

The chain (abbreviated to 'ch') has two main functions in crochet. The first forms the starting point of a piece and is known as the foundation chain. The second allows you to work stitches of different heights and is called a turning chain.

Foundation chain

Foundation chains can be used in two ways. They can act like a 'cast-on' in knitting and form the basis of the first row. Alternatively, one end of the foundation chain can be joined to the other to form a ring, thus allowing you to work in the round.

If you find that your foundation chain is too tight, try working it in a size larger hook; change back down to the recommended size when you start crocheting.

1 With the hook in your right hand and yarn held and tensioned in your left hand, place the hook so it is your side of the yarn and the tip is on its side and facing towards the yarn. Move the hook underneath the yarn and then pull it back towards the loop on the hook. This involves rotating the hook in an anti-clockwise movement so that the tip of the hook is now facing downwards.

2 Keeping a good tension on the tail, pull the yarn gently through the loop on the hook.

3 Once the stitch is complete, the hook can be rotated in a clockwise position until the tip is facing upwards again.

Repeat the steps until you have made the required number of chain, remembering to reposition the finger and thumb that are tensioning the tail as you go to maintain an even tension.

Working into the foundation chain

Once you are ready to start, you will need to work the first row of stitches into the foundation chain. In the illustration here **(1)**, the hook has been inserted into the second chain from the hook – the first stage in making a row of double crochet (US: single crochet) stitches (see p. 24 for a full explanation on making this stitch). Insert the hook into the middle of the 'V' shape created by the chain stitch to start making your stitch.

Subsequent rows **(2)** will be worked by sliding the hook underneath (rather than into) the 'V' shape created by the row of stitches underneath.

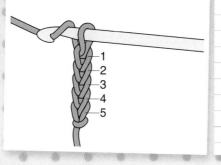

1

1
2
3
4
5

If you find that your foundation chain is too tight, try working it in a size larger hook; change back down to the recommended size when you start crocheting.

Counting chains

Some people find this tricky, so here are a few points to look out for. Crochet chains have a front and a back. The front is smooth and looks like a series of 'V's sitting on top of each other. The back has a ridge of bumps like a spine.

The illustration above **(1)** shows how to count the 'V's on the front of the work.

Remember to push up the slipknot before counting so that this is not included in the stitch count, and ignore the loop on the hook.

Turning chain

Crochet allows you to vary the height or depth of the stitches you work. You have to make preparations at the beginning of each row to make this possible: this means making a turning chain. The chain itself is worked in the usual manner (see p. 16), but the number of chain that you work depends on the stitch that follows the turning chain.

The taller the stitch, the more turning chain need to be worked. The examples here show the four most commonly used crochet stitches.

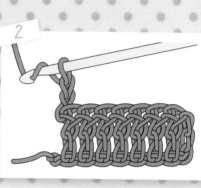

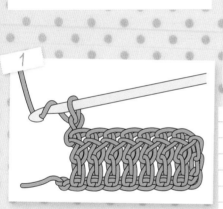

1 Double crochet (US: single crochet)

This is the shortest stitch and requires only 1 turning chain.

2 Half treble crochet (US: half double crochet)

This is the next tallest stitch and so requires 2 turning chain at the beginning of a row.

The turning chain worked for these two stitches does not count as part of the overall stitch count; it is simply there to help you get to the correct height needed to work the stitches of the subsequent row.

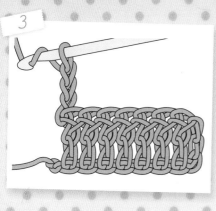

3 Treble crochet (US: double crochet)

This is the first of the taller stitches and requires 3 turning chain at the beginning of a row.

4 Double treble crochet (US: treble crochet)

This is the second of the taller stitches and requires 4 turning chain at the beginning of a row.

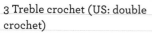

In both of these examples (and for any taller stitches), it becomes necessary to make the turning chain count as if it were a stitch. This is achieved by working the required number of chain and then missing the first stitch of the row. You then continue to work the rest of the row as the pattern describes. When you come to the end of the following row, you will work into the top chain of the turning chain. This achieves two things: the stitch count is restored, and the chains are pulled up to make a straight edge and look like the rest of the stitches worked in that row.

Extra turning chain

Sometimes you will be required to work more turning chain than is directly equivalent to the stitches you are about to work. This typically happens when working a mesh or trellis stitch; the turning chain needs to travel both vertically and horizontally in order to form part of the way the mesh or trellis is constructed. The Elizabeth sofa throw (pp. 52–53) is an example of this.

Turning chain in the round

It is necessary to work a turning chain when working in the round, unless you want to create a spiral. Working chains in the round is described in two ways. If you are working a piece in the round where the right side of the work is always facing you, the chain will be referred to as a starting chain. The motifs in the Little book of shapes (pp. 114–123) are worked in this way. For projects where it is necessary for you to turn the work, the chain will still be referred to as a turning chain.

Slip stitch

The slip stitch (abbreviated to 'ss') has no 'height' as such, but is used to move the working yarn along a piece without cutting and reattaching it. It can also be used to join pieces.

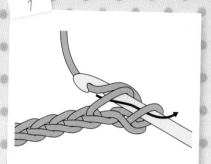

1 Insert the hook through the chain. Draw the yarn around the hook, through the chain and then through the loop on the hook.

If a piece requires you to work a very long foundation chain, you may find it helpful to place stitch markers at certain intervals so you can keep track of where you are.

Double crochet (US: single crochet)

Double crochet (abbreviated to 'dc'/ US: 'sc') requires 1 turning chain. It is the shortest of the crochet stitches and is very commonly used. It creates a dense texture and is often worked on edgings to keep a neat, tight border.

1 Insert the hook into the second chain from the hook. Draw the yarn around the hook and through the chain, so that there are now two loops on the hook.

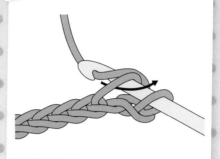

2 Wrap the yarn around the hook again and then draw the yarn through both loops on the hook to complete the stitch.

Half treble crochet
(US: half double crochet)

Half treble crochet (abbreviated to 'htr'/US: 'hdc') requires 2 turning chain. Half treble crochet is the next tallest stitch, begun by wrapping the yarn round the hook once before inserting the hook into the chain.

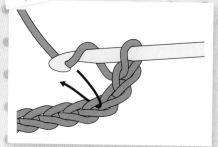

1 Start by wrapping the yarn round the hook. Insert the hook through the third chain from the hook.

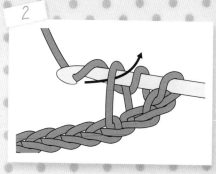

2 Wrap the yarn around the hook again and draw it through the chain so that there are now three loops on the hook.

3 Wrap the yarn around the hook again and then draw the yarn through all three loops to complete the stitch.

Treble crochet (US: double crochet)

Treble crochet (abbreviated to 'tr'/US: 'dc') requires 3 turning chain. Treble crochet is one of the taller stitches, and is commonly used where a more open, lacy-looking fabric is required. It is also frequently used in combinations, to make shell stitches and clusters.

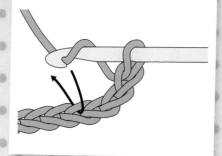

1 Start by wrapping the yarn around the hook. Insert the hook through the fourth chain from the hook.

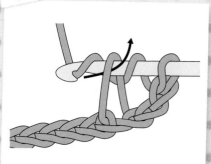

2 Wrap the yarn around the hook again and draw through the chain – there are now three loops on the hook.

3 Wrap the yarn around the hook again and draw it through the first two loops on the hook.

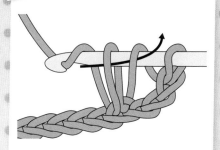

4 Wrap the yarn round the hook again and draw it through the two remaining loops on the hook to complete the stitch.

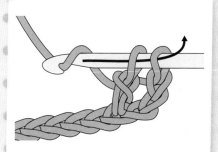

Double treble crochet
(US: treble crochet)

Double treble crochet (abbreviated to 'dtr/US: 'tr') requires 4 turning chain.

1 Start by wrapping yarn around the hook twice. Insert the hook through the fifth chain from the hook.

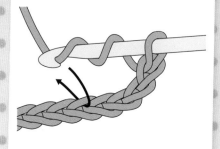

2 Wrap the yarn round the hook again and draw it through the chain – there will be four loops on the hook.

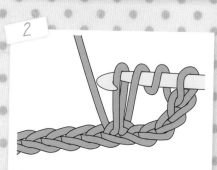

3 Wrap the yarn round the hook and draw through the first two loops – three loops will be left on the hook.

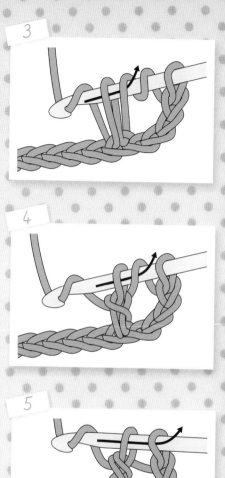

4 Wrap the yarn round the hook and draw through the next two loops; two loops will be left on the hook.

5 Wrap the yarn round the hook a final time and draw the yarn through the remaining two loops to complete the stitch.

Extra-tall stitches

You will now probably be able to work out how to form the taller stitches; for each subsequent 'height' of stitch, just wrap the yarn round the hook one extra time.

Triple treble crochet (abbreviated to 'ttr'/US: double treble crochet, abbreviated to 'dtr'): requires 5 turning chain and is begun with 3 yrh.

Quadruple treble crochet (abbreviated to 'quadtr'/US: triple treble crochet, abbreviated to 'ttr'): requires 6 turning chain and is begun with 4 yrh.

Quintuple treble crochet (abbreviated to 'quintr'/US: quadruple treble crochet, abbreviated to 'quadtr'): requires 7 turning chain and is begun with 5 yrh.

Sextuple treble crochet (abbreviated to 'sextr'/US: quintuple treble crochet, abbreviated to 'quintr'): requires 8 turning chain and is begun with 6 yrh.

The Snooze pet bed (pp. 106–109) features triple treble (US: double treble) and sextuple treble (US: quintuple treble) crochet stitches.

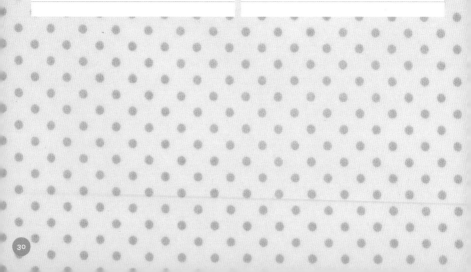

Gallery of techniques

Some of the projects in this book use only the basic stitches explained in the previous pages; others use more complex techniques. These include working in the round, creating texture and lace effects, and beadwork.

Working in the round

Working in the round can be used to create motifs as well as the cylindrical shapes that you might use to make a bag.

All circular motifs or medallions start with a short chain that is joined into a circle. The circle is then built up through a series of evenly spaced increases on each subsequent round. Alternatively, these increases can be grouped in different ways to create different shapes such as hexagons and triangles (as in the Little book of shapes, pp. 114–123). Once you have made the basic ring, the first round will be worked into the ring rather than the chains that it is made up of. Following rows will be worked into spaces or stitches as directed.

Clusters

Clusters are worked in a similar way to internal decreases (see p. 42). They are typically made up of between two and four stitches that are joined together after leaving the last loop of each stitch on the hook and then pulling the yarn through all the remaining loops to complete the stitch. Instructions on how to work a cluster within a pattern will be found in the Special Abbreviations section.

Shells

Shells are worked in a similar way to internal increases (see p. 40) and involve working three or more stitches into a stitch or chain. The shell shape is created by missing out the stitches either side of the shell and working chains in between the groups of stitches.

Puff stitches

Puff stitches are a little more complex to work than clusters (see p. 32), but produce a lovely delicate texture, especially when worked in a fine yarn. Just like clusters, puff stitches are made by working to the last stage of the stitch and pulling the yarn through all the loops that are left on the hook. The difference is that you are working more loops together in a shorter space.

Bobble stitches

This feature is popular in both knitting and crochet, but is much easier to crochet! Bobbles differ from the other techniques described here because they can be worked only on a wrong-side row. Once again, they are worked in a similar way to a cluster, with each stitch being worked to the point where two stitches remain on the hook. The difference is that the stitches used to produce the bobble are trebles (US: doubles), whereas the rest of the row is worked in double crochet (US: single crochet). This helps to create the raised effect. It is important to work the stitch that follows the bobble quite tightly so the bobble stands out as proudly from the surface as possible.

Crossed stitches

In the same way that cabling in knitting transfers the position of certain stitches, so crossing stitches does in crochet. Stitches can be crossed in front of or behind each other and are usually made from trebles (US: doubles). To cross a stitch to the front, you will need to work to where the cross is to be placed and then miss the next stitch. Work a stitch into the next stitch. Continue to work the second stitch by wrapping the yarn around the hook and then inserting it from the front and then into the front of the stitch you have just missed. As you complete the stitch in the usual way, you will find that it has crossed in front of the previous stitch. Crossing a stitch from behind is worked in a similar way except that you will take the hook and yarn behind the first stitch and then insert it into the front of the missed stitch.

Raised stitches

Raised stitches are very clearly defined; they are different from the other techniques because they require you to work around the 'post', or the length of previous stitches, rather than into a stitch or chain. These stitches can be made shorter or longer depending on how many rows deep you place them, but the basic principle is the same. Again, you will need to work to where the stitch is required, wrap the yarn around the hook, and then insert the hook from front to back around the space that is made between the two following stitches. Continue to work the stitch in the usual way.

To work a raised stitch from the back, you will follow the same instructions, but this time insert the hook from back to front around the space that is made between the two following stitches. Take care not to work into any stitches that are covered by a raised stitch.

Lace

Lace tends to be the term that we use for open-work or mesh- and trellis-based stitches. Basic mesh stitches provide you with a framework or grid, created by working into stitches rather than chain spaces. It is often seen in wraps and scarves. This mesh can be embellished with beads, fabric or with more textural stitches. Trellis stitches are created by working into the chain spaces rather than the stitches created by the basic framework. These are very popular stitches for shawls and ponchos.

Both techniques require careful counting, especially when working the foundation chain and the first row.

Beads

Beads make a lovely addition to crochet. The technique is simple to work but highly effective. You will need to start by selecting the right beads for the yarn you are using. As a general rule, size 6 beads will fit most DK-weight (US: light worsted) yarns, while size 8 beads will fit most 4ply-weight (US: sport-weight) yarns. Make sure you have enough beads, and thread them on to your yarn before starting work. Thread up a fine-eyed needle (one that will fit through the centre of the beads) with enough sewing cotton to make a 10cm (4in) loop. Knot the ends and then open up the loop so that you can drop the tail end of the yarn through the loop. You will now be able to slot the beads down the needle, onto the sewing thread and then onto the yarn. (Sequins could be added in the same way.)

In a similar way to working bobbles, beads can be placed only on a wrong-side row, but can be used in conjunction with a variety of stitches and edgings. Beads are often used on a double crochet (US: single crochet)

background. You will simply need to work to where the bead is to be placed, insert the hook through the chain and then pull the bead down the yarn until it sits snugly against the hook, then secure it by working a dc (US: sc) in the normal way. If you were working in treble crochet (US: double crochet), you would place the bead just before the last stage of the stitch was worked.

Shaping crochet pieces

Once you are familiar with the basic crochet stitches, and some of the more advanced stitches, you may want to expand your repertoire by learning how to shape your crochet pieces by increasing and decreasing. This will allow you to make a greater range of projects.

There are two main types of shaping in crochet: internal and external. Internal shaping takes place within a row or round; external shaping takes place at the beginning or end of a row. Both these techniques might be used to make a garment, while internal shaping allows you to create the rippled or undulating patterns that are often associated with crochet.

Increasing within a row

You will need to work to the point in the row or round where the increase is required. If you are increasing by one stitch, then simply work two stitches into the next one **(1)**. If a greater number is required, then work the specified number into the next stitch as before. Diagram **(2)** shows three stitches worked into the next stitch.

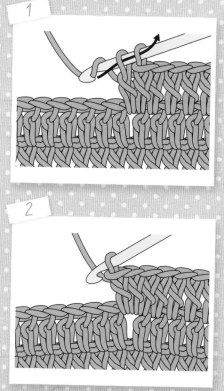

Adding stitches to the right-hand side of the work

If you need to add stitches to the right-hand side of your work, you need to prepare for this at the end of the previous row, by working the required number of chain, plus any turning chain (1). With the RS (right side) of the work facing (2), this leaves you free to work into the increased number of chain.

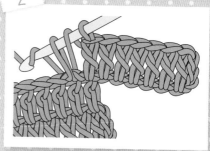

Adding stitches to the left-hand side of the work

Adding stitches to the left-hand side of your work is a little trickier. You will need to work to the end of the row and then place the working stitch onto a stitch holder (1). Join in a new length of the same yarn to the last stitch of this row and then work the required number of chain. Fasten off. Return the working stitch to the hook and then work to the end of the additional chain.

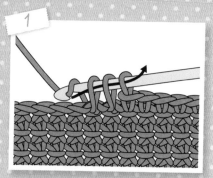

Decreasing within a row

Decreases are made by working one or more stitches together. This is achieved by working to the correct point in the row and then working a stitch in the usual way, but stopping before the last time you take the yarn round the hook. At this stage you start to work the next stitch and then stop at the same point. So if you were working two double crochet (US: single crochet) stitches together (dc2tog/US: sc2tog) – as shown in **(1)** above – you would now have three loops left on the hook. Take the yarn around the hook for the last time and pull through all three loops. Two stitches have become one.

The same principle would apply for decreasing more than one stitch at a time. For example, to work tr3tog (US: dc3tog), you make three incomplete treble crochet (US: double crochet) stitches; when you have four loops left on the hook, you take the yarn round the hook one last time and draw the yarn through all four loops to decrease by two stitches.

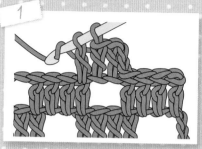

Decreasing stitches at the beginning of a row

This is a lot easier than adding them! If you need to decrease a number of stitches at the beginning of a row, simply work a series of slip stitches equal to the number you want to lose and then work the correct number of turning chain and continue to work to the end of the row. In **(1)** above, the slip stitches used to get to mid-row are essentially invisible; then three treble stitches (US: doubles) have been worked after a 3-chain turning chain.

Decreasing stitches at the end of a row

If you need to decrease a number of stitches at the end of a row, all you need to do is leave that number of stitches unworked. You then continue by turning and working the appropriate turning chain and then carry on as described by the pattern.

Reading a crochet pattern

Patterns often appear to be very densely written, with a seemingly endless trail of abbreviations, brackets and parentheses. However, you will be surprised how quickly you are able to read this 'shorthand' once you have completed a couple of projects. Here are a few pointers to help you on your way.

What you need/Materials

This section describes the amount of yarn, the size of hook or hooks you need, as well as any additional items such as a cushion pad or buttons.

Size

This is where you will find details of how big the finished project should be. In cases where tension (see below) is not so important, an approximate size will be given.

Tension

Tension (US: gauge) is an important piece of information and will often determine the success of your project. A project's tension tells you how many stitches and rows are required to achieve a 10cm (4in) square.

Keep Post-it notes handy so that you can isolate parts of a pattern or chart when concentrating on a certain feature.

The information may relate to a single stitch or the pattern that the project requires.

When you are working a tension square, you should make it slightly larger than 10cm (4in) so that you get a true reading of a 10cm (4in) square. For example, if a pattern determines 16 sts and 20 rows to 10cm (4in) measured over pattern, try working 24 sts and 30 rows in order to make an accurate assessment.

Abbreviations

No one could be expected to learn and remember all the abbreviations that exist. To make things easier, photocopy a list of abbreviations and keep them handy when working on a project.
NB: in this book, we use metric hook sizes first, with US equivalents given in brackets. In the patterns, we give UK crochet stitch names first, with the US equivalents following, separated by a slash.
If you find this confusing to follow, try photocopying the patterns you would like to make and highlighting instructions in the 'language' you are most familiar with.
Below is a list of the abbreviations used in this book:

3-tr cluster = three treble cluster

bch = beaded chain

bdc = beaded double crochet

beg = beginning

ch = chain

cl = cluster

cm = centimetre(s)

dc = double crochet

dc2tog = double crochet the next two stitches together

dc3tog = double crochet the next three stitches together

dtr = double treble

dtr/rf = raised double treble crochet at the front of the fabric

g = gram(s)

htr = half treble

in = inch(es)

LH = left hand

MB = make bobble

mm = millimetre(s)

patt = pattern

rem = remaining

rep = repeat

RH = right hand

RS = right side

sextr/rf = sextuple treble crochet at the front of the fabric

sp = space

ss = slip stitch

st(s) = stitch(es)

tch = turning chain

tog = together

tr = treble

tr2tog = treble the next two stitches together

tr3tog = treble the next three stitches together

tr5tog = treble the next five stitches together

ttr/rb = raised triple treble crochet at the back of the fabric

ttr/rf = raised triple treble crochet at the front of the fabric

WS = wrong side

yrh = yarn round hook

NB: here stitches are listed in order of height from shortest to tallest

UK terms	US conversions
double crochet (dc)	= single crochet (sc)
half treble (htr)	= half double crochet (hdc)
treble (tr)	= double crochet (dc)
double treble (dtr)	= treble (tr)
triple treble (ttr)	= double treble (dtr)
quadruple treble (quadtr)	= triple treble (ttr)
quintuble treble (quintr)	= quadruple treble (quadtr)
sextuple treble (sextr)	= quintuble treble (quintr)

Special abbreviations

Sometimes you will find these at the beginning of a pattern that features a more unusual stitch. This section will also give an explanation of how to work the stitch.

Square and round brackets

It is important to understand the difference between square and round brackets. Square ones are used to contain an instruction that needs to be repeated or a series of stitches that need to be worked into either the same stitch or the same place. Round brackets are used to add extra information such as stitch count. They often appear in a pattern after the turning chain: the information they contain will tell you whether a stitch counts or not or whether it should be used in a particular way; e.g. 5ch (counts as 1tr/1dc and 2ch).

Asterisks

Asterisks perform much the same function as square brackets and usually indicate from where a pattern needs to be repeated.

You may also find a double asterisk in a pattern (**). These will occur within the whole repeat and mark where you need to finish a row or round if the patterning ends halfway through a repeat; e.g. repeat from * twice and then from * to ** once.

Capital letters

Capital letters are also a form of shorthand and are used to denote which colour of yarn to use where more than one colour is used within a pattern (see p. 64, for example).

Before and after care

This is often the part of the project that is overlooked, usually because you are eager to start making something else! However, the preparation and finishing of a project is vital if you are to be completely satisfied with your creation.

Tension (gauge) square

There are several practical reasons for working a tension (US: gauge) square. It allows you to check whether your finished piece will match the size of that of the pattern. It will provide you with a reference if you decide to work in that stitch and yarn in the future. It may tell you that you need to change the style or size of the hook to suit the yarn you have chosen to work with.

Once you have made the square (see p. 44), you will need to lay out the fabric on a flat surface and then, using a tape measure and pins, mark out a 10cm (4in) square. If your tension matches the pattern, you can get started; if not, you may need to adjust your hook size.

Blocking

There is often some confusion as to what blocking is and why we need to do it. One of the main reasons is to encourage the work into its correct shape and to make the sewing up of seams easier.

Start by making sure that the yarn you have used is suitable for blocking. You will find this information on the ball band.

Once you have established this and taken note of the correct heat setting, carefully pin out your work onto a padded board (an ironing board is fine), with the wrong side facing you. This is the best time to ease the piece into shape and smooth out any wrinkles. Avoid placing the full weight of your iron onto your work; it is much better to let the iron hover over the surface. Also, never drag the iron across the work; move it around the work.

It is not always advisable to block your work in this way. The yarn may not be suitable, or you may risk flattening raised or textured stitches. In these cases, you will need to 'wet' block the piece instead. Prepare the work in the same way as above, but instead of using an iron, lay a clean damp cloth over your work and leave it until dry.

In both cases, do not remove the pins until your work is dry.

Continuing to care

When you have finished your project, it is a good idea to keep one of the yarn labels in your sketchbook or notebook. This will act as a reference when you need to check for washing or dry-cleaning instructions. If your project needs to be hand-washed, make sure that you use an appropriate detergent and squeeze the water out gently. Do not be tempted to wring the water out,

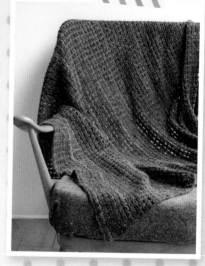

as this could distort the shape of your work.

Finally, find a suitable place to dry your work. It will need to be out of direct sunlight and large enough to lay your work out flat.

Home

Elizabeth sofa throw

Cosy mesh-stitch throw in autumnal colours

Materials
Nine 50g (135m/148yd) balls of Rowan Colourspun (or equivalent yarn: DK/light worsted wool and mohair blend) in variegated reds and browns
4.00mm (US: G-6) hook

Size
Approx. 110 x 110cm (43¼ x 43¼in)

Tension (Gauge)
20 sts and 18 rows to 10cm (4in) using a 4.00mm (US: G-6) hook and measured over pattern

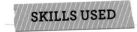

SKILLS USED

· Working turning chains
· Making mesh stitches
· Keeping an even tension

Using 4.00mm (G-6) hook, ch 234.
Foundation Row: 1tr/1dc into 10th ch from hook, *ch3, miss 3ch, 1tr/1dc into next ch; rep from * to end of row, turn.
Row 1 (WS): Ch1, 1dc/1sc into first tr/dc, *ch3, miss 3ch, 1dc/1sc into next tr/dc; rep from * to end of row, ending final repeat with ch3, miss 3ch, 1dc into 3rd of 10ch.
Row 2: Ch6 (counts as 1tr/1dc and ch3), miss the first dc/sc and ch3, 1tr/1dc into next dc/sc, *ch3, miss next 3ch, 1tr/1dc into next dc/sc; rep from * to end, turn.
The last 2 rows form the pattern and should be repeated until work measures approx. 110cm (43¼in), ending with a row 2.
Fasten off.

Finishing
Weave in any loose ends and press according to ball band instructions.

Birdhouse

Crochet house with button and embroidery details

Materials

Rowan Handknit Cotton (85m/93yd per 50g ball; or equivalent yarn: DK/light worsted 100% cotton):
Two balls in ochre (A)
One ball in ecru (B)
One ball in dark purple (C)
Tiny amount of fresh green (D) for embroidery
3.00mm (US: C-2/D-3) and 3.50mm (US: E-4) crochet hooks
1 large and 2 smaller square buttons for windows
6 flower-shaped buttons (I used 3 lilac and 3 gold)

1 small bead for door handle
Upholstery foam cut to size
Piece of felt measuring 14 x 16cm (5½ x 6¼in)

Size

Approx. 14cm (5½in) wide, 16cm (6¼in) deep and 20cm (8in) high at tallest point

Tension (Gauge)

20 sts and 23 rows to 10cm (4in) using a 3.50mm (US: E-4) hook and measured over double crochet (US: single crochet).

Sides (both alike)

Using 3.00mm (C-2/D-3) hook and yarn A, work 4 ch and join with ss to form a ring.
Round 1: Ch3 (counts as 1tr/1dc), 15tr/15dc into the ring, join with ss to 3rd of 3ch. Fasten off. (16 tr/16 dc)
Round 2: Join yarn B into sp between any 2tr/2dc, ch3 (counts as 1tr/1dc), 1tr/1dc into the same sp, 2tr/2dc in every rem sp between 2tr/2dc, change to yarn

SKILLS USED

- Shaping and joining crochet pieces
- Working crochet motifs
- Adding embroidered details

C when joining with ss to 3rd of 3ch. Fasten off. (32 tr/32 dc)

Round 3: Ch3 (counts as 1tr/1dc), 1tr/1dc into same place, 1tr/1dc into next tr/dc, [2tr/2dc into next tr/dc, 1tr/1dc into next tr/dc] fifteen times, join with ss to 3rd of 3ch. Fasten off. (48 tr/48 dc)

Round 4: Join yarn A to any tr/dc, ch4 (counts as 1dtr/1tr), [2tr/2dc, 2ch, 2tr/2dc, 1dtr/1tr] into same place, *miss next 2tr/2dc, 1htr/1hdc into each of next 2tr/2dc, 1dc/1sc into each of next 3tr/3dc, 1htr/1hdc into each of next 2tr/2dc, miss next 2tr/2dc, **[1dtr/1tr, 2tr/2dc, 2ch, 2tr/2dc, 1dtr/1tr] into next tr/dc; rep from * twice and from * to ** once more, join with ss to 4th of 4ch. Fasten off.

Round 5: Join yarn B to any ch-2 corner sp, ch3 (counts as 1tr/1dc), [2dtr/2tr, 2ch, 2dtr/2tr, 1tr/1dc] into same sp, *1tr/1dc into next 12tr/12dc, **[1tr/1dc, 2dtr/2tr, 2ch, 2dtr/2tr, 1tr/1dc] into next ch-2 corner sp; rep from * twice and from * to ** once more, join with ss to 3rd of 3ch. Fasten off.

Round 6: Join yarn C to any ch-2 corner sp, ch3 (counts as 1tr/1dc), [1tr/1dc, 2ch, 2tr/2dc] into same sp, *1tr/1dc into next 17tr/17dc, **[2tr/2dc, 2ch, 2tr/2dc] into

next ch-2 corner sp; rep from * twice and from * to ** once more, changing to yarn A when joining with ss to 3rd of 3ch.

Round 7: Ch3 (counts as 1tr/1dc), 1tr/1dc into each tr/dc of previous round, working 5tr/5dc into each ch-2 corner sp, join with ss to 3rd of 3ch. Fasten off. (100 tr/100 dc)

Front

Using 3.50mm (E-4) hook and B ch 28.

Row 1 (RS): 1dc/1sc in 2nd ch from hook, 1dc/1sc in every rem ch to end of row, turn. (27 dc/27 sc)

Row 2: Ch1 (does not count as st), 1dc/1sc in every dc/sc to end of row, turn.

Repeat row 2 until work measures 13cm (5in) and ending on a RS row.

SHAPING

Row 1: Ch1, dc2tog/sc2tog over next 2dc/2sc, dc/sc in every remaining dc/sc to last 2 sts, dc2tog/sc2tog over last 2 sts, turn.

Repeat last row until 3 sts remain.

Next row: Dc3tog/sc3tog. Fasten off.

Back

Work as for Front using yarn C.

Roof panels (both alike)

Using 3.50mm (E-4) hook and yarn A, ch 30.

Row 1 (RS): 1dc/1sc in 2nd ch from hook, 1dc/1sc into every rem ch to end of row, turn. (29 dc/29 sc)

Row 2: Ch1, 1dc/1sc in first dc/sc, *ch1, miss a st, 1dc/1sc into next dc/sc; rep from * to end, turn.

Row 3: Ch1, 1dc/1sc in first dc/sc, *1tr/1dc in next ch-1 sp, 1dc/1sc in next dc/sc; rep from * to end of row.

Rep last 2 rows, seven more times.
Fasten off.

Door

Using 3.50mm (E-4) hook and yarn C, ch10.

Row 1 (RS): 1dc/1sc in 2nd ch from hook, 1dc/1sc in every rem ch to end of row, turn. (9 dc/9 sc)

Row 2: Ch1 (does not count as st), 1dc/1sc in every dc/sc to end of row, turn.

Rep row 2, twelve more times.
Fasten off.

Finishing

Weave in any loose ends and press according to the ball band instructions. Using the photos as a guide, slipstitch door into place and sew on window buttons and bead for door handle. Work stems of chain stitch to form stems of flowers and then stitch flower buttons to the top.

Start to build the house by placing wrong sides of front of house and a side panel together. Join both pieces of fabric together with a ss, ch1, 1dc/1sc into same place and then continue to join both pieces of fabric with a double crochet (single crochet) seam. Fasten off.

Continue to join the other side piece and the back piece in the same way until all four 'walls' are seamed together.

Use the same method to join the two roof panels together, working 2dc/2sc into last dc/sc, turn. (30 dc/30 sc).

Picot edge (ridge tiles): Using 3.50mm (E-4) hook and yarn A, *ch3, join with ss into the back of the first of 3ch, miss next dc/sc, 1ss into next dc/sc; rep from * to end of row. Fasten off.

Join row ends of roof to apex of front and back of structure, using a dc/sc seam. There will be a slight overhang at the sides, so slipstitch the underneath of the eaves to the top edge of the sides.

Cut foam to size. Place construction over the foam and then slipstitch felt base to four foundation edges.

My inspiration for this project was to bring the natural world into the home. The emphasis here is on fun rather than function, and I had a great time thinking of little details to make the house look like a real home. The use of buttons and simple embroidery complement the crocheted structure and help bring the house to life. There is lot of scope for you to make this design your own, whether for yourself or a feathered friend!

Homespun table runner

Simple table runner worked in basic crochet stitches

Materials
Ten 50g (85m/93yd) balls of Rowan
Handknit Cotton (or equivalent yarn:
DK/light worsted 100% cotton)
in burnt orange
4.00mm (US: G-6) hook

Size
Approx. 104 x 62cm (41 x 24½in)

Tension (Gauge)
16 sts and 12 rows to 10cm (4in) using
4.00mm (US: G-6) hook and measured
over pattern.

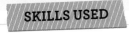

SKILLS USED

· Working the longer crochet
  stitches
· Making mesh stitches
· Keeping an even tension

Using 4.00mm (G-6) hook, ch 164.

Row 1: 1dc/1sc in 2nd ch from hook,
1dc/1sc in every ch to end of row, turn.
(163 sts)

Row 2: Ch1 (does not count as st),
1dc/1sc in every dc/sc to end of
row, turn.

Row 3: Ch1 (does not count as st),
1dc/1sc in every dc/sc to end of
row, turn.

Row 4: Ch1 (does not count as st),
1dc/1sc in every dc/sc to end of
row, turn.

Row 5: Ch2 (does not count as st),
1htr/1hdc in every dc/sc to end of
row, turn.

Row 6: Ch2 (does not count as st),
1htr/1hdc in every htr/hdc to end of
row, turn.

Row 7: Ch3 (counts as first tr/dc), miss
first htr/hdc, 1tr/1dc in every rem htr/
hdc to end of row, turn.

Row 8: Ch3 (counts as first tr/dc), miss
first tr/dc, 1tr/1dc in every tr/dc to

end of row, ending with 1tr/1dc in 3rd of 3ch, turn.

Row 9: Ch4 (counts as 1tr/1dc and 1ch), miss first tr/dc, [1tr/1dc in next tr/dc, ch1, miss next tr/dc] ending with 1tr/1dc in 3rd of 3ch, turn.

Row 10: Ch3 (counts as 1tr/1dc), miss first tr/dc, [1tr/1dc in ch-1 sp, 1tr/1dc in next tr/dc] ending with 1tr/1dc in 3rd of 3ch, turn.

Row 11: As row 8.

Row 12: Ch2 (does not count as st), 1htr/1hdc in every tr/dc to end of row, turn.

Row 13: As row 6.

Row 14: Ch1 (does not count as st), 1dc/1sc in every htr/hdc to end of row, turn.

Rows 15–27: As rows 1–13.

Rows 28–29: As rows 7–8.

Row 30: Ch3 (counts as 1tr/1dc), miss next tr/dc, 1tr/1dc in next tr/dc, *ch3, miss next 3tr/3dc, 1tr/1dc in each of next 3tr/3dc; rep from * to last 5tr/5dc, ch3, miss next 3tr/3dc, 1tr/1dc in next tr/dc, 1tr/1dc in 3rd of 3ch, turn.

Row 31: Ch4 (counts as 1tr/1dc and ch1), 3tr/3dc in next ch-3 loop, *ch3, 3tr/3dc in next ch-3 loop; rep from * to last ch-3 loop, ch1, 1tr/1dc in 3rd of 3ch, turn.

Row 32: Ch3 (counts as 1tr/1dc), 1tr/1dc in next ch-1 sp, *ch3, 3tr/3dc in next ch-3 loop; rep from * to last ch-3 loop, ch3, miss next 3tr/3dc, 1tr/1dc in ch-1 sp of the turning chain, 1tr/1dc in 3rd of 3ch, turn.

Row 33: Ch3 (counts as 1tr/1dc), miss first tr/dc, 1tr/1dc in next tr/dc, *3tr/3dc in next ch-3 loop, 1tr/1dc in each of next 3tr/3dc; rep from * across to ch-3 loop, ending with 1tr/1dc in last tr/dc and 1tr/1dc in 3rd of 3ch, turn.

Rows 34–35: Ch3 (counts as 1tr/1dc), miss first tr/dc, 1tr/1dc in every tr/dc to end of row, ending with 1tr/1dc in 3rd of 3ch, turn.

Rows 36–46: As rows 30–35 and then rows 30–34 once more.

Row 47: As row 12.

Row 48: As row 6.

Row 49: As row 7.

Row 50: As row 8.

Row 51: As row 9.

Row 52: As row 10.

Row 53: As row 11.

Row 54: As row 12.

Row 55: As row 13.

Row 56: As row 14.

Row 57: As row 4.
Row 58: As row 5.
Rows 59–69: As rows 48–58. Fasten off.

Finishing
Weave in any loose ends and press
according to ball band instructions.

This table runner is an ideal first
project, as it will help you to become
familiar with the basic stitches and
will demonstrate how the turning
chain works. It is worked in a good-
quality pure cotton yarn that shows
up the stitch work beautifully, and
would look equally at home in the
dining room or on the picnic table.

Lucienne oblong cushion

Retro-style cushion using interlocking colours

Materials

Two 50g (120m/131yd) balls of Amy Butler Belle Organic DK in aubergine (A)
One 50g (120m/131yd) ball of Amy Butler Belle Organic DK in pale blue (B)
One 50g (85m/93yd) ball of Rowan Handknit Cotton in deep blue (C)
One 50g (120m/131yd) ball of Amy Butler Belle Organic DK in yellow green (D)
One 50g (120m/131yd) ball of Amy Butler Belle Organic DK in green (E)
(or equivalent yarns: DK/light worsted 100% cotton and 50% cotton/50% wool blend)
4.00mm (US: G-6) crochet hook
40 x 30cm (15¾ x 12in) cushion pad

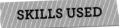

SKILLS USED

- Changing colours
- Crocheting seams together
- Adapting a colour scheme

Size

Approx. 40 x 30cm (15¾ x 12in)

Tension (Gauge)

18 sts x 10 rows to 10cm (4in) using a 4.00mm (US: G-6) hook and measured over pattern.

Special abbreviations

Tr2tog (US: dc2tog) = treble (US: double crochet) the next 2 stitches together
Tr3tog (US: dc3tog) = treble (US: double crochet) the next 3 stitches together

Pattern note

Change colour at last yrh (yarn round hook) of preceding row before turning.

Front

Using 4.00mm (G-6) hook and A, ch 57.
Foundation Row (WS): Miss first 2ch (counts as 1htr/1hdc), 1htr/1hdc into next ch, *miss 1ch, [1htr/1hdc, 1ch, 1htr/1hdc] into next ch; rep from * to last 2ch, miss 1ch, 2htr/2hdc into last ch, turn.

Row 1: Using B, 3ch, 1tr/1dc into first st (counts as tr2tog/dc2tog), *1ch, tr3tog/dc3tog into next ch space; rep from * to last space, ending 1ch, tr2tog/dc2tog into 3rd of 3ch, turn.

Row 2: Using C, 2ch (counts as 1htr/1hdc), miss first st, *work [1htr/1hdc, 1ch, 1htr/1hdc] into next ch space; rep from * ending 1htr/1hdc into 2nd of 2ch, turn.

Row 3: Using D, 3ch (counts as 1tr/1dc), miss first st, *tr3tog/dc3tog into next sp, 1ch; rep from * to last ch space, tr3tog/dc3tog into last ch space, 1tr/1dc into 3rd of 3ch, turn.

Row 4: Using E, 2ch (counts as 1htr/1hdc), 1htr/1hdc into first st, *work [1htr/1hdc, 1ch, 1htr/1hdc] into next ch space; rep from * ending 2htr/2hdc into 2nd of 2ch, turn.

Row 5: As row 1 using A.

Row 6: As row 2 using B.

Row 7: As row 3 using C.

Row 8: As row 4 using D.

Row 9: As row 1 using E.

Row 10: As row 2 using A and changing to B at last yrh.

Row 11: 2ch, 1htr/1hdc into every st along the row, turn.

Rows 12–19: As row 11.

Row 20: As row 2 in A.

Row 21: As row 3 in E.

Row 22: As row 4 in D.

Row 23: As row 1 in C, changing to yarn B at last yrh.

Rows 24–29: As row 11. Fasten off.

Back

Using 4.00mm (G-6) hook and yarn A, ch 57.

Foundation Row: 1htr/1hdc into 3rd ch from hook, 1htr/1hdc in every ch to end of row, turn. (55 ch)

Row 1: 2ch (does not count as st), 1htr/1hdc into every htr/hdc to end of row, turn.

Repeat row 1 until work measures the same as Front. Fasten off.

Making up

Weave in any loose ends. With wrong sides together, join yarn A to top RH corner with a ss. Ch1, 1dc/1sc in same place, work a further 2dc/2sc into same place (corner made). Continue to work a dc/sc border through both pieces of fabric, working 3dc/3sc into next two corners, insert cushion pad and close open seam with dc/sc border as before.

Kaleidoscope circular cushion

Round cushion with varied motifs worked in a fine cotton yarn

Materials

Two 50g (140m/153yd) balls of Rowan Siena 4 Ply (or equivalent yarn: 4ply/sport-weight 100% mercerized cotton) in each of:

Aqua (A)
Sky blue (B)
Dark green (C)
3.00mm (US: C-2/D-3) hook
30cm (12in) circular cushion pad

Size

Approx. 30cm (12in) in diameter

Tension (Gauge)

24 sts and 9 rows to 10cm (4in) using 3.00mm (US: C-2/D-3) hook and measured over treble crochet (US: double crochet).

Special abbreviations

Beg cl = beginning cluster made from 2 treble stitches (US: 2 double crochet stitches)

Cl = cluster made from 3 treble stitches (US: 3 double crochet stitches)

Dc2tog (US: sc2tog) = Double crochet (US: single crochet) the next 2 stitches together

Puff st = [yrh, insert hook into foundation ring, draw up loop] twice, yrh, draw loop through all 5 loops on hook

Front

Centre motif (make 1):

Using 3.00mm (C-2/D-3) hook and yarn A, ch4 and join with a ss to form a ring. Round 1: Ch3, 1htr/1hdc into ring (counts as first puff st), ch1, [puff st into ring, ch1] seven times, join with ss to top of first puff st.

SKILLS USED

· Making circular crochet motifs
· Working cluster and puff stitches
· Joining motifs together

Round 2: Ss to next ch sp, ch3, 1tr/1dc into ch sp at base of ch3, ch2, [2tr/2dc into next ch-1 sp, ch2] seven times, join with ss to top of beg 3ch.

Round 3: Ss to next ch sp, ch3, [1tr/1dc, ch1, 2tr/2dc, ch2] into ch sp at base of ch3, ch2, *[2tr/2dc, ch1] twice into next ch-2 sp; rep from * six times more, join with ss to top of beg 3ch. Break A.

Round 4: Join yarn B. Ch3, 2tr/2dc into ch sp at base of ch3, ch1, [3tr/3dc into next ch-1 sp, ch1] fifteen times, join with ss to top of beg 3ch. Break B.

Round 5: Join yarn C. Ch3, 3tr/3dc into ch sp at base of ch3, ch1, [4tr/4dc into next ch-1 sp, ch1] fifteen times, join with ss to top of beg 3ch.

Round 6: Ch1 (counts as first dc/first sc), 1dc/1sc into each tr/dc and ch sp to end of round, join with a ss to 1ch at beg of round. Fasten off.

Flower motif (make 3):

Using 3.00mm (C-2/D-3) hook and yarn C, ch6, join with a ss to form a ring.

Round 1: Ch4 (counts as first dtr/first tr), 2dtr/2tr into ring, [ch1, 3dtr/3tr into ring] five times, changing to yarn A when joining with a ss to top of 4ch, turn. (Break C).

Round 2: Ss into first ch-1 sp, ch7, [1dc/1sc into next ch-1 sp, ch6] five times, join with a ss to beg ch-1 sp. Do not turn.

Round 3: Ss into first ch-6 sp, [1htr/1hdc, 2tr/2dc, 3dtr/3tr, 2tr/2dc, 1htr/1hdc] into each ch-6 sp, changing to yarn B when joining with ss to first htr/first hdc of a petal, turn. (Break C).

Round 4: Ch4 (counts as first dtr/first tr), *1tr/1dc into each of next 2tr/2dc, 1htr/1hdc into each of next 3dtr/3tr, 1tr/1dc into each of next 2tr/2dc, 1dtr/1tr into each of next htr/hdc; rep from * five times more, missing last dtr/last tr of final repeat and joining with a ss to top of 4ch.

Round 5: Ch3 (counts as 1tr/1dc), 1tr/1dc into base of ch3, 1tr/1dc into next st, [2tr/2dc into next st, 1tr/1dc into next st] to end of round, join with ss to top of 3ch. Fasten off.

Cluster circle (make 3):

Using 3.00mm (C-2/D-3) hook and yarn B, ch4 and join with a ss to form a ring.

Round 1: Ch1, 6dc/6sc into the ring, join with a ss to first dc/first sc.

Round 2: Ch1, 2dc/2sc into next dc/sc, six times, join with a ss to first dc/first sc. (12 dc/12 sc)

Round 3: Ch1, 2dc/2sc into next dc/sc, twelve times, join with a ss to first dc/first sc. (24 dc/24 sc). Break yarn B.

Round 4: Join yarn C to any dc/sc from previous round, ch3 (counts as 1tr/1dc), beg cl into same dc/sc, ch2, miss next dc/sc, *cl into next dc/sc, ch2, miss next dc/sc; rep from * ten times, join with ss to top of beg cl.

Round 5: Ss along to next ch-2 sp, ch3 (counts as 1tr/1dc), beg cl into same sp, ch3, *cl into next ch-2 sp, ch3; rep from * ten times, changing to yarn A when joining with a ss to top of beg cl. Break yarn C.

Round 6: Ch3, 2tr/2dc into top of beg cl, 3tr/3dc into next ch-3 sp, *3tr/3dc into top of next cl, 3tr/3dc into next ch-3 sp; rep from * ten times, join with a ss to 3rd of 3ch. Fasten off. Weave in any loose ends and press according to ball band instructions.

Back

Using 3.00mm (C-2/D-3) hook and yarn A, ch6 and join with a ss to form a ring. Stripe sequence:

A
B
C

(Remember to change yarn at last yrh of each round.)

Round 1: Ch3 (counts as 1tr/1dc), 15tr/15dc into the ring, join with ss to 3rd of 3ch. (16 tr/16 dc)

Round 2: Ch3 (counts as 1tr/1dc), 1tr/1dc into same place, 2tr/2dc into each tr/

each dc of previous round, join with ss to 3rd of 3ch. (32 tr/32 dc)

Round 3: Ch3 (counts as 1tr/1dc), 1tr/1dc into same place, *[1tr/1dc into next tr/dc, 2tr/2dc into next tr/dc]; rep from * to last st, 1tr/1dc into last st, join with ss to 3rd of 3ch. (48 tr/48 dc)

Round 4: Ch3 (counts as 1tr/1dc), 1tr/1dc into same place, *[1tr/1dc into each of next 2tr/2dc, 2tr/2dc into next tr/dc]; rep from * to last 2 sts, 1tr/1dc into each of last 2 sts, join with ss to 3rd of 3ch. (64 tr/64 dc)

Round 5: Ch3 (counts as 1tr/1dc), 1tr/1dc into same place, *[1tr/1dc into each of next 3tr/3dc, 2tr/2dc into next tr/dc]; rep from * to last 3 sts, 1tr/1dc into each of last 3 sts, join with ss to 3rd of 3ch. (80 tr/80 dc)

Round 6: Ch3 (counts as 1tr/1dc), 1tr/1dc into same place, *[1tr/1dc into each of next 4tr/4dc, 2tr/2dc into next tr/dc]; rep from * to last 4 sts, 1tr/1dc into each of last 4 sts, join with ss to 3rd of 3ch. (96 tr/96 dc)

Round 7: Ch3 (counts as 1tr/1dc), 1tr/1dc into every tr/dc to end of round, join with ss to 3rd of 3ch.

Round 8: Ch3 (counts as 1tr/1dc), 1tr/1dc into same place, *[1tr/1dc into each of

next 5tr/5dc, 2tr/2dc into next tr/dc]; rep from * to last 5 sts, 1tr/1dc into each of last 5 sts, join with ss to 3rd of 3ch. (112 tr/112 dc)

Round 9: As round 7.

Round 10: Ch3 (counts as 1tr/1dc), 1tr/1dc into same place, *[1tr/1dc into each of next 6tr/6dc, 2tr/2dc into next tr/dc]; rep from * to last 6 sts, 1tr/1dc into each of last 6 sts, join with ss to 3rd of 3ch. (128 tr/128 dc)

Round 11: As round 7.

Round 12: Ch3 (counts as 1tr/1dc), 1tr/1dc into same place, *[1tr/1dc into each of next 7tr/7dc, 2tr/2dc into next tr/dc]; rep from * to last 7 sts, 1tr/1dc into each of last 7 sts, join with ss to 3rd of 3ch. (144 tr/144 dc)

Round 13: As round 7.

Round 14: Ch3 (counts as 1tr/1dc), 1tr/1dc into same place, *[1tr/1dc into each of next 8tr/8dc, 2tr/2dc into next tr/dc]; rep from * to last 8 sts, 1tr/1dc into each of last 8 sts, join with ss to 3rd of 3ch. (160 tr/160 dc)

Round 15: Ch3 (counts as 1tr/1dc), 1tr/1dc into same place, *[1tr/1dc into each of next 9tr/9dc, 2tr/2dc into next tr/dc]; rep from * to last 9 sts, 1tr/1dc into each of last 9 sts, join with ss to

3rd of 3ch. (176 tr/176 dc)
Weave in any loose ends and press all pieces according to ball band instructions.

Making up
FRONT
Arrange Flower and Cluster motifs equally around edge of Centre motif. Attach by slipstitching 5ch from each motif to the Centre motif. Join the sides of each motif around the centre by missing 5 sts and then slipstitching together the next 10ch from each circle. You will find that the Cluster circles are slightly smaller than the Flower motifs. Using 3.00mm (C-2/D-3) hook and yarn C, join with ss to point where slipstitching ends.

Half round: Ch1, 1dc/1sc into same place, 1htr/1hdc into next st, 1tr/1dc into every tr/dc until you are 3 sts away from where slipstitching begins again, 1htr/1hdc into next st, 1dc/1sc into next st, ss into last st, fasten off.
Repeat for remaining 2 Cluster circles.
Joining round: With RS facing of any Floral motif and using 3.00mm (C-2/D-3) hook and yarn A, join with a ss

to 10th ch from where slipstitching ends, ch1, 1dc/1sc into same place, 1dc/1sc into next 29 sts, ch10, *join to next motif as before with a dc/sc, 1dc/1sc into next 22 sts, ch10, join to next motif as before with a dc/sc, 1dc/1sc into next 29 sts, ch10; rep from * once more, join to next motif as before with a dc/sc, 1dc/1sc into next 22 sts, ch10, join with a ss to first dc/first sc.
Final round: Ch3 (counts as 1tr/1dc), 1tr/1dc into every rem dc/sc of the round and working 10tr/10dc into ch-10 sp, join with ss to 3rd of 3ch.
Fasten off and weave in any further loose ends.
Press if required.

JOINING FRONT AND BACK
Using 3.00mm (C-2/D-3) hook and yarn B, insert hook through both pieces of fabric and join with a ss. Ch1, 1dc/1sc in same place, continue to work 1dc/1sc into corresponding stitches (working dc2tog/sc2tog where necessary to ensure a good fit) around the edge of the circle until you reach the halfway point, insert cushion pad, and then continue as before until round is complete. Join with a ss to first dc/first sc. Fasten off.

Tranquil bed runner

Undulating bed throw with beaded decoration

Materials

Seven 50g (113m/123yd) balls of Rowan Wool Cotton in pale lilac (A)

Three 25g (210m/229yd) balls of Rowan Kidsilk Haze in pale pink (B)

Two 50g (113m/123yd) balls of Rowan Wool Cotton in dark purple (C)

(or equivalent yarns: DK/light worsted 50% cotton/50% merino wool blend, and 4ply/sport-weight super kid mohair and silk blend)

4.00mm (US: G-6) hook

672 size 6 beads in amethyst (96 beads are used for each of the 7 bead rows)

Size

Approx. 154 x 34cm (60½ x 13½in)

Tension (Gauge)

17 sts and 13 rows to 10cm (4in) using a 4.00mm (US: G-6) hook and measured over pattern.

Special abbreviations

Bdc (US: bsc) = beaded double crochet (US: beaded single crochet); see p. 39 for more on crocheting with beads

Htr3tog (US: hdc3tog) = half treble (US: half double crochet) the next 3 stitches together

Tr2tog (US: dc2tog) = treble (US: double crochet) the next 2 stitches together

Pattern note

Thread 96 beads onto yarn at the beginning of row 4 and for each repeat of row 4 (there are seven bead rows in total).

SKILLS USED

- Crocheting with beads
- Forming a ripple stitch with decreases
- Changing colours

Using 4.00mm (G-4) hook and yarn A, ch 291.

Row 1 (RS): 1tr/1dc in 4th ch from hook, [tr2tog/dc2tog over next 2ch] twice, *[ch1, htr3tog/hdc3tog into next ch] five times, 1ch, **[tr2tog/dc2tog over next 2ch] six times; rep from * ending last rep at ** when 6ch remain, [tr2tog/dc2tog over next 2ch] three times, turn.

Row 2: Ch1, 1dc/1sc into first st and into each st and ch-1 sp to end of row, excluding the 3ch missed at the beginning of the previous row, turn.

Row 3: Ch3, miss first st, 1tr/1dc into next st, [tr2tog/dc2tog over next 2 sts] twice, *[ch1, htr3tog/hdc3tog into next st] five times, 1ch, **[tr2tog/dc2tog over next 2 sts] six times; rep from * ending last rep at ** when 6 sts remain, [tr2tog/dc2tog over next 2ch] three times, miss 3ch, turn.

Row 4: Ch 1, 1dc/1sc into each of first 3 sts, *[1dc/1sc into next ch-1 sp, 1dc/1sc into next st] five times, 1dc/1sc into next ch-1 sp, 1bdc/1bsc into each of next 6 sts; rep from * to last 8 sts, [1dc/1sc into next ch-1 sp, 1dc/1sc into next st] five times, 1dc/1sc into next ch-1 sp, 1dc/1sc into each of last 3 sts.

Row 5: As row 3, changing to yarn B at last yrh.

Row 6: As row 2.

Row 7: As row 3, changing to yarn C at last yrh.

Row 8: As row 2.

Rows 3–8 form the pattern and should be repeated five more times, observing the colour changes set out above.

Rows 39–41: As rows 3–5, omitting colour changes.

Rows 42–43: As rows 2–3. Fasten off.

Finishing

Weave in any loose ends.

Edges (both worked the same):

With RS of work facing and using 4.00mm (G-4) hook, join yarn A to corner with a ss.

Row 1: Ch1, 1dc/1sc into same place, work a further 63dc/63sc evenly across row ends, turn.

Row 2: Ch1, 1dc/1sc into every dc/sc to end of row, turn.

Row 3: Ch1 [1dc/1sc into next dc/sc, ch2, miss next 2dc/2sc] to last dc/sc, 1dc/1sc into last dc/sc, changing to yarn C at last yrh.

Row 4: Ch3 (counts as 1tr/1dc), 2tr/2dc into next ch-2 sp, [3tr/3dc into next ch-2 sp] to end of row, ss to turning ch.

Fasten off.

Weave in any loose ends and press according to ball band instructions.

I wanted to create something very gentle and feminine with this design. The muted palette and soft rippling pattern create a soothing piece of crochet, while the beads add a hint of glamour. You will soon get into the rhythm of the two-row pattern, although it is important to keep a check on your counting because of the length of the rows. I think this piece would look delicious laid out on crisp white cotton bedlinen, but you could alter the emphasis of the yarns and beads to suit the colours in your own boudoir.

Accessories

Millie slouchy hat

Cosy chic hat with lacy panels

Materials

Two 50g (140m/153yd) balls of Rowan
Kid Classic (or equivalent yarn: aran/
worsted-weight lambswool and kid
mohair blend) in camel
5.00mm (US: H-8) hook

Size

Approx. 50 x 32cm (19¾ x 12½in) – fits
an average-size adult head

Tension (Gauge)

18 sts and 9 rows to 10cm (4in) using a
5.00mm (US: H-8) hook and measured
over pattern.

SKILLS USED

- Shaping crochet with decreases
- Making lacy stitches
- Working in the round

Special abbreviations

Dc2tog (US: sc2tog) = double crochet
(US: single crochet) the next 2 stitches
together

Tr2tog (US: dc2tog) = treble (US: double
crochet) the next 2 stitches together

Hat

Using 5.00mm (H-8) hook, ch 96 and
join with a ss to form a ring, taking care
not to twist the work.

Round 1: Ch3 (counts as 1tr/1dc), 1tr/1dc
in each of next 4ch, *ch2, miss next 5ch,
(1tr/1dc, ch1, 1tr/1dc, ch1, 1tr/1dc, ch1,
1tr/1dc) in next ch, ch2, miss next 5ch,
1tr/1dc in each of next 5ch; rep from * to
last 5ch, ch2, ss to 3rd of 3ch.

Round 2: Ch3 (counts as 1tr/1dc), 1tr/1dc
in each of next 4tr/4dc, *ch2, miss next
ch-2 sp, (1tr/1dc, ch3, 1tr/1dc) in each
of next ch-1 sp, ch2, miss next ch-2 sp,
1tr/1dc in each of next 5tr/5dc; rep from *
to last ch-2 sp, ch2, ss to 3rd of 3ch.

Round 3: Ch3 (counts as 1tr/1dc), 1tr/1dc
in each of next 4tr/4dc, *ch2, miss next 2

sp, (1tr/1dc, ch1, 1tr/1dc, ch1, 1tr/1dc, ch1, 1tr/1dc) in next ch-3 loop, ch2, miss next 2 sp, 1tr/1dc in each of next 5tr/5dc; rep from * end of round, ch2, ss to 3rd of 3ch. Rounds 2–3 form the pattern. Repeat six more times and then repeat round 2 once more.

Shape crown
Round 17: Ch3 (counts as 1tr/1dc), 1tr/1dc in each of next 2tr/2dc, tr2tog/dc2tog, *ch2, miss next 2 sp, (1tr/1dc, ch1, 1tr/1dc, ch1, 1tr/1dc, ch1, 1tr/1dc) in next ch-3 loop, ch2, miss next 2 sp, 1tr/1dc in each of next 3tr/3dc, tr2tog/dc2tog; rep from * end of round, ch2, join with ss to 3rd of 3ch. (90 sts)
Round 18: Ch3 (counts as 1tr/1dc), tr2tog/dc2tog, 1tr/1dc in next tr/dc, *ch2, miss next ch-2 sp, (1tr/1dc, ch3, 1tr/1dc) in each of next ch-1 sp, ch2, miss next ch-2 sp, tr2tog/dc2tog, 1tr/1dc in next 2tr/2dc; rep from * to last ch-2 sp, ch2, join with ss to 3rd of 3ch. (84 sts)
Round 19: Ch3 (counts as 1tr/1dc), tr2tog/dc2tog, *ch2, miss next 2 sp, (1tr/1dc, ch1, 1tr/1dc, ch1, 1tr/1dc, ch1, 1tr/1dc) in next ch-3 loop, ch2, miss next 2 sp, tr2tog/dc2tog; rep from * end of round, ch2, join with ss to 3rd of 3ch. (78 sts)
Round 20: Ch3 (counts as 1tr/1dc), *miss next ch-2 sp, (1tr/1dc, ch3, 1tr/1dc) in each of next ch-1 sp, miss next ch-2 sp; rep from * to last ch-2 sp, miss last ch-2 sp, join with ss to 3rd of 3ch.
Round 21: Ch3 (counts as 1tr/1dc), *(1tr/1dc, ch1, 1tr/1dc) into second ch-3 loop, 1tr/1dc into next tr/dc; rep from * to end of round, join with ss to 3rd of 3ch. (24 sts)
Round 22: Ch1, 1dc/1sc into same place, 1dc/1sc in every st to end of round, join with a ss to first dc/sc. (24 dc/24 sc)
Round 23: Ch1, dc2tog/sc2tog across the round, join with ss to first dc/sc. (12 dc/12 sc)
Round 24: Ch1, dc2tog/sc2tog across the round, join with ss to first dc/sc. (6 dc/6 sc)
Fasten off.
Thread yarn back through these 6 sts, pull up tight and fasten off securely.

Band
Using 5.00mm (H-8) hook, rejoin yarn to foundation chain with a ss.
Round 1: Ch1, 1dc/1sc into same place,

This slouchy hat is an ideal project for extending your pattern-reading and shaping skills. Its construction means that you can become familiar with the pattern repeat before you have to start shaping the hat, which then makes the shaping easier to understand. For a less slouchy version, work fewer repeats of the pattern before shaping the crown, or try working a summer version in a cotton equivalent.

1dc/1sc into every ch along the round, join with a ss to first dc/sc. (96 dc/96 sc)

Round 2: Ch1, 1dc/1sc into back loop only of every dc/sc to end of round, join with a ss to first dc/sc.

Round 3: As round 2.

Round 4: Ch1, 1dc/1sc into same place, *dc2tog/sc2tog, 1dc/1sc in next dc/sc; rep from * to end of round. (64 dc/64 sc) Fasten off.

Finishing

Weave in any loose ends and press lightly according to ball band instructions.

Oscar man's scarf

Simply smart scarf for a stylish gentleman

Materials

Four 100g (115m/126yd) balls of Rowan Cocoon (or equivalent yarn: chunky/bulky-weight merino wool and kid mohair blend) in green
6.00mm (US: J-10) hook

Size

Approx. 17 x 172cm (6¾ x 67¾in)

Tension (Gauge)

14 sts x 20 rows to 10cm (4in) using a 6.00mm (US: J-10) hook and measured over pattern.

The sophisticated rib pattern is produced by simply working into the back loop only of rows of double crochet (US: single crochet). This look, combined with the luxury yarn, makes it an ideal gift for the man who thinks he has everything!

SKILLS USED

- Making a ribbed pattern
- Working into the back loop of a stitch
- Keeping an even tension

Using 6.00mm (J-10) hook, ch 248.
Row 1: 1dc/1sc into 2nd ch from hook, 1dc/1sc in every ch to end, turn.
Row 2: Ch1 (does not count as st), 1dc/1sc into back loop only of each dc/sc to end of row, turn.
Row 2 forms the pattern and should be repeated until work measures 17cm (6¾in), or desired width.
Fasten off.

Finishing

Weave in any loose ends. There is no need to press the piece, as this will flatten the rib pattern.

Amanda frilled snood

Glamorous two-tone neck warmer in pretty lace and ruffles

Materials

Two 50g (140m/153yd) balls of Rowan
Kid Classic (or equivalent yarn: (aran/
worsted-weight lambswool and kid
mohair blend) in deep blue (A)
One 25g (210m/229yd) ball of Rowan
Kidsilk Haze (or equivalent yarn: 4ply/
sport-weight super kid mohair and silk
blend) in sky blue (B) (used double
throughout)
5.00mm (US: H-8) hook

Size

Approx. 58cm (23in) in circumference,
22cm (8½in) deep excluding frill

SKILLS USED

· Crossing stitches to make a lace
  pattern
· Crocheting in rounds
· Making a ruffled edging

Tension (Gauge)

14 sts and 8 rows to 10cm (4in) using
5.00mm (US: H-8) hook and measured
over pattern.

Snood

Using 5.00mm (H-8) hook and yarn
A, ch 94, join with a ss to form a ring,
taking care not to twist.

Round 1: Ch3 (counts as 1tr/1dc), miss
1ch, 1tr/1dc in every ch to end of the
round, join with ss to 3rd of 3ch.

Round 2: Ch3 (counts as 1tr/1dc), miss
next tr/dc, *miss next tr/dc, 1tr/1dc in
next tr/dc, 1tr/1dc in the tr/dc you have
just missed (this will feel as if you are
working backwards, but it is how the cross
is made); rep from * to last tr/dc, 1tr/1dc in
last tr/dc, join with ss to 3rd of 3ch.

Round 3: Ch4 (counts as 1tr/1dc, ch1),
*(1tr/1dc, ch1) between the 2tr/2dc of the
next crossed tr/dc, skip next 2tr/2dc; rep
from * to last tr/dc, miss last tr/dc and
join with ss to 3rd of 4ch.

Round 4: Ch3 (counts as 1tr/1dc), *miss the next ch-1 sp, 1tr/1dc in next ch-1 sp, 1tr/1dc in the ch-1 sp you have just missed (crossed treble/crossed double crochet is made); rep from * to end of round, join with ss to 3rd of 3ch.

Round 5: Ch3 (counts as 1tr/1dc), miss first tr/dc, 1tr/1dc in every tr/dc to end of round, joining with ss to 3rd of 3ch.

Repeat rounds 2–5, three more times. Fasten off.

Frill
NECK EDGE
Round 1: Using 5.00mm (H-8) hook and yarn B double, join with a ss to first tr/dc of final round, ch1, 2dc/2sc in same place, 2dc/2sc in every tr/dc to end of round, join with ss to first dc/sc.

Round 2: Ch1, 2dc/2sc in same place, 2dc/2sc in every dc/sc of previous round, join with ss to first dc/sc. Fasten off.

LOWER EDGE
Repeat as for neck edge.

Finishing
Weave in any loose ends. Press very lightly according to ball band instructions and taking care to avoid the frill.

Emma wristwarmers

Cosy mittens with pretty bobble pattern

Materials

Two 50g (100m/109yd) balls of Rowan
Baby Alpaca DK (or equivalent yarn:
DK/light worsted 100% alpaca) in blue
4.00mm (US: G-6) hook

Size
Small (Medium) adult

The Small size pair illustrated are
approx. 20cm (8in) in circumference
and 15cm (6in) from wrist to fingertip;
Medium size are approx. 23.5cm (9¼in)
in circumference and the same depth
from wrist to fingertip

Tension (Gauge)

18 sts and 13 rows to 10cm (4in) using
4.00mm (US: G-6) hook and measured
over pattern.

Special abbreviations

Dtr/rf (US: tr/rf) = raised double treble
crochet (US: raised treble crochet) at
the front of the fabric: Wrap the yarn
around the hook, insert the hook from

in front and from right to left around the
stem of the appropriate stitch, and then
complete the stitch in the usual way
MB = make bobble stitch from 5 treble
(US: double crochet) stitches
Tr2tog (US: dc2tog) = treble (US: double
crochet) the next 2 stitches together

Pattern notes

The instructions for the panel pattern
are as follows:
Row 1 (RS): 1tr/1dc into each of next 4
sts, [1ch, miss 1st st, 1tr/1dc into next st]
three times, 1tr/1dc into each of last 3 sts.
Row 2: 1dc/1sc into each of first 4tr/4dc,
work MB into next ch sp, 1dc/1sc into
next tr/dc, 1dc/1sc into next sp, 1dc/1sc
into next tr/dc, MB into next sp, 1dc/1sc
into each of last 4tr/4dc.
Row 3: 1dtr/rf/1tr/rf around the st,
two rows below, 1tr/1dc into next st on
previous row, 1dtr/rf/1tr/rf around next
st two rows below, [1ch, miss a stitch,
1tr/1dc into next st on previous row]
three times, 1ch, miss a st, 1dtr/rf/1tr/rf

around next st two rows below, 1tr/1dc into next st on previous row, 1dtr/rf/1tr/rf around the next st two rows below.

Row 4: 1dc/1sc into each of next 6 sts, MB into next tr/dc, 1dc/1sc in remaining 6 sts.

Row 5: [1dtr/rf/1tr/rf around corresponding raised st two rows below, 1tr/1dc into next st] twice, [ch1, miss a st, 1tr/1dc into next st] three times, 1dtr/rf/1tr/rf around corresponding st two rows below, 1tr/1dc into next st, 1dtr/rf/1tr/rf around corresponding st two rows below.

Right mitt

Using 4.00mm (G-6) hook, ch 36(42) and join with ss to form a ring, taking care not to twist the chain.

Round 1: Ch1 (does not count as a st), 1dc/1sc into every ch, join with a ss to first dc/sc. (35(41) sts)

Round 2: Ch3 (counts as 1tr/1dc), miss next dc/sc, 1tr/1dc in every dc/sc to end of round, join with a ss to 3rd of 3ch.

Round 3: Ch1 (does not count as a st), 1dc/1sc into every tr/dc, join with a ss to first dc/sc.

Round 4: As round 2.

Round 5: As round 3.

Round 6 (thumbhole): Ch3 (counts as 1tr/1dc), 1tr/1dc in next 3(4)dc/3(4)sc, ch4(5), miss 4(5) sts, 1tr/1dc in next 3(4) dc/3(4)sc, work row 1 of panel patt over next 13 sts, 1tr/1dc in each remaining dc/sc to end of round, join with a ss to 3rd of 3ch, turn.

Round 7 (wrong side of work is now facing): Ch1 (does not count as a st), 1dc/1sc into next 11(14)tr/11(14)dc, work row 2 of panel patt over next 13 sts, 1dc/1sc into next 3(4)tr/3(4)dc, 4(5) dc/4(5)sc into 4(5)ch-sp, 1dc/1sc into last 4(5)tr/4(5)dc, join with a ss to first dc/sc, turn.

Round 8: Ch3 (counts as 1tr/1dc), 1tr/1dc in next 11(14)dc/11(14)sc, work row 3 of panel patt over next 13 sts, 1tr/1dc in remaining 11(14)dc/11(14)sc, join with a ss to 3rd of 3ch, turn.

Round 9: Ch1 (does not count as a st), 1dc/1sc into next 11(14)tr/11(14)dc, work row 4 of panel patt over next 13 sts, 1dc/1sc into next 11(14)tr/11(14)dc, join with a ss to first dc/sc, turn.

Round 10: Ch3 (counts as 1tr/1dc), 1tr/1dc in next 11(14)dc/11(14)sc, work row 5 of panel patt over next 13 sts, 1tr/1dc in next 1(2)dc/1(2)sc, 2tr/2dc in next dc/sc, 1tr/1dc in next 6(7)dc/6(7)sc, 2tr/2dc in next dc/sc, 1tr/1dc in last 1(2)dc/1(2)sc, join with a ss to 3rd of 3ch, turn. (37(43) sts)

Round 11: Ch1 (does not count as a st), 1dc/1sc into next 13(16)tr/13(16)dc, work row 2 of panel patt over next 13 sts, 1dc/1sc into next 11(14)tr/11(14)dc, join with a ss to first dc/sc, turn.

Round 12: Ch3 (counts as 1tr/1dc), 1tr/1dc in next 11(14)dc/11(14)sc, work row 3 of panel patt over next 13 sts, 1tr/1dc in next 1(2)dc/1(2)sc, tr2tog/dc2tog over next 2dc/2sc, 1tr/1dc in next 6(7)dc/6(7)sc, tr2tog/dc2tog over next 2dc/2sc, 1tr/1dc in last 1(2)dc/1(2)sc, join with a ss to 3rd of 3ch, turn. (35(41) sts)

Round 13: As round 9.

Round 14: As round 10.

Round 15: As round 11.

Rounds 16–19: Ch1 (does not count as a st), 1dc/1sc into every st, join with a ss to first dc/sc, turn at end of round 19 so that WS of work is facing.

Round 20: Ch1 (does not count as a st), [1dc/1sc in next 2dc/2sc, MB using 3 treble crochet/double crochet sts in next dc/sc] to last 2 sts, 1dc/1sc in next 2dc/2sc, join with ss to first dc/sc, turn.

Rounds 21–23: As round 16. Fasten off.

Left mitt

Work as for Right Mitt for rounds 1–5.

Round 6 (thumbhole): Ch3 (counts as 1tr/1dc), 1tr/1dc in next 11(14)dc/11(14)sc, work row 1 of panel patt over next 13 sts, 1tr/1dc in next 3(4)dc/3(4)sc, ch4(5), miss 4(5) sts, 1tr/1dc in next 3(4)dc/3(4)sc, join with a ss to 3rd of 3ch, turn.

Round 7 (wrong side of work is now facing): Ch1 (does not count as a st), 1dc/1sc into next 3(4)tr/3(4)dc, 4(5) dc/4(5)sc into 4(5)ch-sp, 1dc/1sc into last 4(5)tr/4(5)dc, work row 2 of panel patt over next 13 sts, 1dc/1sc into next 11(14)tr/11(14)dc, join with a ss to first dc/sc, turn.

Round 8: Ch3 (counts as 1tr/1dc), 1tr/1dc in next 11(14)dc/11(14)sc, work row 3 of panel patt over next 13 sts, 1tr/1dc in rem 11(14)dc/11(14)sc, join with a ss to 3rd of 3ch, turn.

Round 9: Ch1 (does not count as a st), 1dc/1sc into next 11(14)tr/11(14)dc, work row 4 of panel patt over next 13 sts, 1dc/1sc into next 11(14)tr/11(14)dc, join with a ss to first dc/sc, turn.

Round 10: Ch3 (counts as 1tr/1dc), 1tr/1dc in next 1(2)dc/1(2)sc, 2tr/2dc in next dc/sc, 1tr/1dc in next 6(7)dc/6(7)sc, 2tr/2dc in next dc/sc, 1tr/1dc in next 1(2) dc/1(2)sc, work row 5 of panel patt over next 13 sts, 1tr/1dc in next 11(14)dc/11(14)

sc, join with a ss to 3rd of 3ch, turn. (37(43) sts)

Round 11: Ch1 (does not count as a st), 1dc/1sc into next 11(14)tr/11(14)dc, work row 2 of panel patt over next 13 sts, 1dc/1sc into next 13(16)tr/13(16)dc, join with a ss to first dc/sc, turn.

Round 12: Ch3 (counts as 1tr/1dc), 1tr/1dc in next 1(2)dc/1(2)sc, tr2tog/ dc2tog over next 2dc/2sc, 1tr/1dc in next 6(7)dc/6(7)sc, tr2tog/dc2tog over next 2dc/2sc, 1tr/1dc in next 1(2)dc/1(2)sc, work row 3 of panel patt over next 13 sts, 1tr/1dc in next 11(14)dc/11(14)sc, join with a ss to 3rd of 3ch, turn. (35(41) sts)

Finishing

Weave in any loose ends and press very lightly according to ball band instructions and avoiding bobbles.

These little handwarmers are deliciously soft! Although this is a small-scale project, it requires a number of skills, including making bobbles, working raised stitches and simple shaping. I think these mitts would make a great winter gift and so have provided two sizes to choose from.

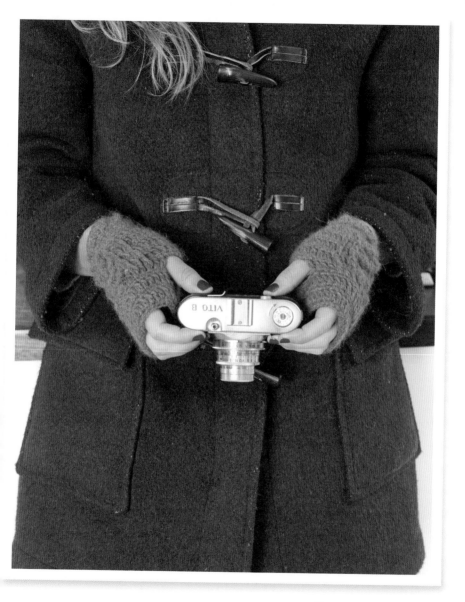

Dorothy headband

Bunny band with crocheted flower and vintage button

Materials

One 50g (90m/98yd) ball of Rowan All Seasons Cotton (or equivalent yarn: DK/light worsted cotton and acrylic blend) in red
5.00mm (US: H-8) hook
Button for decoration

Size

One size fits average head; approx 56cm (22in) circumference and 8cm (3in) wide

Tension (Gauge)

Achieving an exact tension is not vital with this project – it is more important that the band fits your head!

SKILLS USED

- Working in the round
- Creating and filling in chain arches
- Working into chain spaces

Headband

Using 5.00mm (H-8) crochet hook, work 80 foundation ch.

Row 1: 2tr/2dc into 4th ch from hook, *miss 1ch, 2tr/2dc into next ch; rep from * to last 2ch, miss 1ch, 1tr/1dc into last ch, turn.

Row 2: 3ch, *miss 2 sts, 2tr/2dc between the last skipped st and the next st, (this means that you will be working into the middle of the pairs of trebles/double crochet sts on the previous row); rep from * to last 2 sts, miss 1 st, 1tr/1dc into last st, turn.

Row 3: As row 2, but work the last tr/dc into 3rd of 3ch.
Repeat row 3, four more times.
Fasten off.

Flower

Using 5.00mm (H-8) hook, ch6 and join with ss to form a ring.

Round 1: Ch3 (counts as first tr/dc), 1tr/1dc into ring, [ch6, 3tr/3dc into ring] five times, ch6, 1tr/1dc into ring, join with ss to 3rd of 3ch.

Round 2: *Ch1, [1dc/1sc, 1htr/1hdc, 7tr/7dc, 1htr/1hdc, 1dc/1sc] into next ch-6 sp, ch1, miss next tr/dc, ss into next tr/dc; rep from * four more times, ch1, [1dc/1sc, 1htr/1hdc, 7tr/7dc, 1htr/1hdc, 1dc/1sc] into next ch-6 sp, ch1, miss next tr/dc, join with ss to base of beg 1ch. Fasten off.

Finishing

Weave in any loose ends.

Band

With right sides of work together, join back seam using a ss. Attach flower to front, then stitch button to centre of flower.

This design was created in response to three young women I once stood next to on a train platform. One of them was wearing a crocheted bunny band that she had just bought and all three girls were discussing how they could go about making their own. Here is a solution to their dilemma!

Harriet clutch bag

Pretty cotton clutch bag with beaded trim

Materials

Two 50g (85m/93yd) balls of Rowan Handknit Cotton (or equivalent yarn: DK/light worsted 100% cotton) in deep pink

3.50mm (US: E-4) hook

67 size 6 beads in bronze (rows 2 and 4 of the edging require 16 beads each; row 6 requires 35 beads)

Size

Approx. 20 x 15cm (8 x 6in)

Tension (Gauge)

16 sts and 12 rows to 10cm (4in) using a 3.50mm (US: E-4) hook and measured over half treble (US: half double) crochet.

SKILLS USED

- Joining crochet seams
- Working a lacy border
- Crocheting with beads

Special abbreviations

beaded ch = beaded chain. Push bead up close to the hook and work a chain in the usual way

bdc = beaded double crochet (US: bsc = beaded single crochet);
see p. 39 for more on crocheting with beads

Clutch

Using 3.50mm (E-4) hook, ch 38.

Row 1 (RS): 1dc/1sc in 2nd ch from hook, 1dc/1sc in every ch to end, turn.

Row 2: Ch1 (does not count as st), 1dc/1sc in every dc/sc to end of row, turn.

Row 3: Ch2 (does not count as st), 1htr/1hdc in every dc/sc to end of row, turn.

Row 4: Ch2 (does not count as st), 1htr/1hdc in every htr/hdc to end of row, turn.

Repeat row 4 until the work measures 30cm (12in) and ending on a WS row.

A clutch bag is always useful. The half treble (US: half double) fabric is enhanced by the beaded lace-edge trim. I have used bronze beads on a deep pink yarn for a sophisticated palette, but this design could be worked in many different combinations. It is a good idea to try out several different colours of beads before starting your project.

Edging

Row 1 (RS): Ch1 (does not count as st), 1dc/1sc in every htr/hdc to end of row, turn.

Row 2: Ch1 (does not count as st), 1dc/1sc in each of next 2dc/2sc, [bdc/bsc into next dc/sc, 1dc/1sc into next dc/sc] to last 3 sts, bdc/bsc into next st, 1dc/1sc into each of remaining 2dc/2sc, turn.

Row 3: Ch6, 1tr/1dc into first dc/sc, *[miss next dc/sc, 1tr/1dc into next dc/sc] twice, ch3, 1tr/1dc into next dc/sc; rep from * to end, turn.

Row 4: Ch1, [bdc/bsc, ch3, bdc/bsc] into first ch-3 sp, *ch5, [bdc/bsc, ch3, bdc/bsc] into next ch-3 sp; rep from * working last [bdc/bsc, ch3, bdc/bsc] into ch-6 loop, turn.

Row 5: Ch1, 1dc/1sc into first ch-3 loop, *ch4, 1dtr/1tr into next ch-5 loop, ch4, 1dc/1sc into next ch-3 loop; rep from * to end, turn.

Row 6: [1dc/1sc, bdc/bsc, 1dc/1sc, bdc/bsc, 1dc/1sc] into first ch-4 loop, *ch2, 1 beaded ch, ch2, [1dc/1sc, bdc/bsc, 1dc/1sc, bdc/bsc, 1dc/1sc] into next 2 ch-4 loops; rep from * ending with ch2, 1 beaded ch, ch2, [1dc/1sc, bdc/bsc, 1dc/1sc, bdc/bsc, 1dc/1sc] into last 2 ch-4 loop.
Fasten off.

Finishing

Weave in any loose ends and press according to ball band instructions, taking care with the beads and lace points. With right sides together, fold the foundation edge over so that it forms a pocket measuring 12cm (4¾in) deep. Join the sides using backstitch.

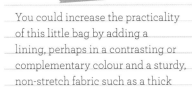

You could increase the practicality of this little bag by adding a lining, perhaps in a contrasting or complementary colour and a sturdy, non-stretch fabric such as a thick cotton. This will help the bag to keep its shape and not distort the fabric. You might also want to secure the closure with the addition of a button and button loop or a snap fastener.

Family

Camilla the cat

Cute cat toy in colourful stripes

Materials
Rowan All Seasons Cotton (90m/98yd per 50g ball; or equivalent yarn: DK/light worsted cotton and acrylic blend):
One ball in dark brown (A)
One ball in light brown (B)
One ball in red (C)
4.00mm (US: G-6) and 10.00mm (US: N/P-15) hooks
Enough toy stuffing to stuff toy firmly
Two buttons for eyes and one for the nose

Size
Approx. 20 x 34cm (8 x 13½in)

SKILLS USED

- Shaping in crochet
- Working in stripes
- Adding sewn-on embellishments

Tension (Gauge)
13 sts and 14 rows to 10cm (4in) using 4.00mm (US: G-6) hook and measured over double crochet (US: single crochet).

Pattern note
The stripe sequence is worked in the following order:
A
B
C

Back
*Using 4.00mm (G-6) hook and yarn A, ch 26.
Row 1: 1dc/1sc in 2nd ch from hook, 1dc/1sc in every ch to end of row, changing to yarn B at last yrh, turn. (25 dc/25 sc)
Row 2: Ch1, 1dc/1sc in every dc/sc to end of row, turn.
Keeping stripe sequence as set, and changing yarns when necessary, rep row 2 until twelve repeats of the three-row stripe sequence have been completed.*

Shaping

(Continue to repeat colour changes for stripe sequence.)

Row 1 (RS): Ch1, dc2tog/sc2tog over next 2dc/2sc, 1dc/1sc in every dc/sc to last 2dc/2sc, dc2tog/sc2tog over last 2dc/2sc, turn. (23 dc/23 sc)

**Row 2 and every foll alt WS row: Ch1, 1dc/1sc in every dc/sc to end of row, turn.

Row 3: Ch1, dc2tog/sc2tog over next 2dc/2sc, 1dc/1sc in every dc/sc to last 2dc/2sc, dc2tog/sc2tog over last 2dc/2sc, turn. (21 dc/21 sc)

Row 5: Ch1, 1dc/1sc in every dc/sc to end of row, turn.

Row 7: Ch1, dc2tog/sc2tog over next 2dc/2sc, 1dc/1sc in every dc/sc to last 2dc/2sc, dc2tog/sc2tog over last 2dc/2sc, turn. (19 dc/19 sc)

Row 9: Ch1, dc2tog/sc2tog over next 2dc/2sc, 1dc/1sc in every dc/sc to last 2dc/2sc, dc2tog/sc2tog over last 2dc/2sc, turn. (17 dc/17 sc)

Row 11: Ch1, dc2tog/sc2tog over next 2dc/2sc, 1dc/1sc in every dc/sc to last 2dc/2sc, dc2tog/sc2tog over last 2dc/2sc, turn. (15 dc/15 sc)

Row 12: Ch1, 1dc/1sc in every dc/sc to end of row, turn.

Row 13: Ss across first 2 sts, ch1, 1dc/1sc in every rem dc/sc to end of row, turn. (13 dc/13 sc)

Row 14: Ss across first 2 sts, ch1, 1dc/1sc in every rem dc/sc to end of row, turn. (11 dc/11 sc)**

Row 15: Ch1, 1dc/1sc in every dc/sc to end of row. Fasten off.

Front

Work as Back from * to *.
Break yarns A and C and continue in yarn B from ** to **.
Break yarn B and join in yarn A.
Row 15: Ch1, 1dc/1sc in every dc/sc to end of row. Fasten off.

Ears (both alike)

Using 4.00mm (G-6) hook and yarn A, ch10.
Row 1: 1dc/1sc in 2nd ch from hook, 1dc/1sc in every ch to end of row, turn. (9 dc/9 sc)
Row 2: Ch1, 1dc/1sc in every dc/sc to end of row, turn.
Row 3: Ch1, dc2tog/sc2tog over next 2dc/2sc, dc/sc in every rem st to last 2dc/2sc, dc2tog/sc2tog, turn. (7dc/7 sc)
Row 4: Ch1, dc2tog/sc2tog over next 2dc/2sc, dc/sc in every rem st to last 2dc/2sc, dc2tog/sc2tog, turn. (5 dc/5 sc)
Row 5: Ch1, dc2tog/sc2tog over next 2dc/2sc, dc/sc in every rem st to last 2dc/2sc, dc2tog/sc2tog, turn. (3 dc/3 sc)
Row 6: Dc3tog/sc3tog. Fasten off.

Tail

Using 10.00mm (N/P-15) hook and four strands of yarn A held together, ch21. Fasten off.

Finishing

Weave in any loose ends. Using the photograph as a guide, attach the eyes and nose. Use yarn A to stitch the whiskers and mouth. Place the right sides of work together and join using backstitch, leaving the base open. Turn right side out and stuff the toy until firm but not over-full. Slipstitch the base seam together. Attach tail to the bottom left-hand edge.

This is a fun project that brings the concept of crocheted toys right up to date. The stripes enable you to be thrifty and use up yarn left over from other projects. Some simple shaping and embroidery will challenge you at the same time. If you want to give Camilla a curlier tail, you could try crocheting around a pipecleaner.

Snooze pet bed

Tartan-inspired floor cushion

Materials
Rowan All Seasons Cotton (90m/98yd per 50g ball; or equivalent yarn: DK/ light worsted cotton and acrylic blend):
Six balls in dark brown (A)
Seven balls in light brown (B)
Six balls in red (C)
5.00mm (US: H-8) hook
71 x 71cm (28 x 28in) cushion pad

Size
Approx. 71 x 71cm (28 x 28in)

SKILLS USED

· Making very long raised stitches
· Working a colour sequence
· Seaming crocheted pieces
  together

Tension (Gauge)
14 sts and 16 rows to 10cm (4in) using 5.00mm (US: H-8) hook and measured over pattern.

Special abbreviations
Sextr/rf (US: quin tr/rf) (raised sextuple treble/US: raised quintuple treble at the front of the fabric) = yarn round hook 6 times, insert the hook from in front and from right to left around the stem of the designated stitch, and complete the stitch in the usual way
Ttr/rb (US: dtr/rb: (raised triple treble/ US: raised double treble at the back of the fabric) = yarn round hook 3 times, insert the hook from behind and from right to left around the stem of the designated stitch, and complete the stitch in the usual way
Ttr/rf (US: dtr/rf) (raised triple treble/ US: raised double treble at the front of the fabric) = yarn round hook 3 times, insert the hook from in front and from right to left around the stem of the

designated stitch, and complete the stitch in the usual way

Pattern note
If you find that the raised stitches are too loose, try working a quin tr/rf (US: quad tr/rf) instead, and work this together with the corresponding dc from the row below to neaten up the top of the stitch.

Front
Using 5.00mm (H-8) hook and yarn A, ch 89.
Foundation Row 1: 1dc/1sc in 2nd ch from hook, 1dc/1sc in every ch to end of row, turn.
Foundation Row 2: Ch1, 1dc/1sc in every dc/sc to end of row, changing to yarn B at last yrh, turn.

Pattern
Row 1: Using yarn B, rep foundation row 2 twice.
Row 3: Using yarn C, rep foundation row 2 four times.
Row 7: Using B, 1ch, 1dc/1sc into each of first 5 sts, *[1ttr/rf/1dtr/rf around corresponding st 5 rows below] twice, 1dc/1sc in next 4 sts, [1ttr/rf/1dtr/rf around corresponding st 5 rows below] twice, 1dc/1sc in next 2 sts; rep from * to last 3 sts, 1dc/1sc in each remaining dc.
Row 8: Using yarn B, rep foundation row 2.
Row 9: Using A, 1ch, 1dc/1sc into each of first 3 sts, *[1sextr/rf/1quintr/rf around corresponding st 9 rows below] twice, 1dc/1sc in next 8 sts; rep from * to last 5 sts, [1sextr/rf/1quintr/rf around corresponding st 9 rows below] twice, 1dc/1sc in each remaining 3dc/3sc.
Row 10: Using yarn A, rep foundation row 2.

Repeat ten-row pattern until work is square and ending on a row 2. Fasten off.

Back

Using 5.00mm (H-8) hook and yarn A, ch 89.

Row 1: 1dc/1sc in 2nd ch from hook, 1dc/1sc in every ch to end of row, turn.

Row 2: Ch 1, 1dc/1sc in every ch to end of row, turn.

Stripe sequence:

2 rows in B.

4 rows in C.

2 rows in B.

2 rows in A.

Repeating row 2 throughout, complete the ten-row stripe sequence, eleven times. Fasten off.

Finishing

Weave in any loose ends and press according to ball band instructions, taking care not to flatten the raised stitches. Place wrong sides of the front and back together and tack along three sides, leaving the base of the cover open (this is a temporary sewn seam to keep the pieces in place until you crochet them together).

Using a 5.00mm (H-8) hook and yarn A, join both pieces of fabric with a ss to bottom right-hand corner, ch1, 1dc/1sc in same place, continue to work through both pieces of fabric using dc/sc to join the seams and remembering to work 3dc/3sc into corners.

Insert cushion pad and join base seam as before.

Fasten off.

The idea of a tartan rug for a pet to snuggle up on was the inspiration for this design. The tartan effect is surprisingly easy to achieve, with raised stitches being used to create the pattern rather than using more than one colour in a row. This cushion would not look out of place in your sitting room; not only will your pet be delighted, but you may find the odd teenager trying to use it too!

Patchwork playball

Crochet motifs create an intriguing stuffed toy

Materials

One 50g (140m/153yd) ball of Rowan
Siena 4 Ply (or equivalent yarn: 4ply/
sport-weight 100% cotton yarn) in each of:
White (A)
Pink (B)
Yellow (C)
Beige (D)
Sky blue (E)
3.00mm (US: C-2/D-3) hook
Toy stuffing
Old pair of tights to contain the stuffing

Size

Approx. 18 x 18cm (7 x 7in) at widest
points

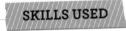

SKILLS USED

· Making crochet motifs
· Joining motifs together
· Stuffing a crocheted piece to
  shape it

Tension (Gauge)

Tension is not important for this project,
as long as all the motifs are worked
to the same tension so that they fit
together neatly.

Pattern note

You will need to make 12 pentagons
using the following colour sequences:
Motif 1: All rounds worked in B.
Motif 2: All rounds worked in C.
Motif 3: All rounds worked in E.
Motif 4: Round 1 in B, round 2 in A,
round 3 in D, round 4 in A.
Motif 5: Round 1 in C, round 2 in A,
round 3 in D, round 4 in A.
Motif 6: Round 1 in E, round 2 in A,
round 3 in D, round 4 in A.
Motif 7: Round 1 in A, round 2 in D,
round 3 in B, round 4 in D.
Motif 8: Round 1 in A, round 2 in D,
round 3 in C, round 4 in D.
Motif 9: Round 1 in A, round 2 in D,
round 3 in E, round 4 in D.
Motif 10: Round 1 in D, round 2 in B,

round 3 in A, round 4 in B.

Motif 11: Round 1 in D, round 2 in C, round 3 in A, round 4 in C.

Motif 12: Round 1 in D, round 2 in E, round 3 in A, round 4 in E.

Basic motif

Foundation ring: Using 3.00mm (C-2/D-3) hook, ch5, join with ss to first ch to form a ring.

Round 1: Ch3 (counts as 1tr/1dc), 1tr/1dc into ring, [ch1 (counts as a corner), 2tr/2dc into ring] four times, ch1, join with ss to top of ch3. (At this point you should have 5 ch-1 spaces.)

Round 2: Ch3 (counts as 1tr/1dc), [1tr/1dc, ch1, 2tr/2dc] into ch-1 sp at base of ch3, ch1, *[2tr/2dc, ch1 (counts as corner), 2tr/2dc] into next ch-1 sp, ch1; rep from * three times more, join with ss to top of ch3. (10 ch-1 spaces)

Round 3: Ch3 (counts as 1tr/1dc), [1tr/1dc, ch1 (counts as corner), 2tr/2dc] into ch-1 sp at base of ch3, *ch1, 2tr/2dc in next ch-1 sp, ch1, [2tr/2dc, ch1 (counts as corner), 2tr/2dc] into next ch-1 sp; rep from * three times more, ch1, 1tr/1dc into next ch-1 sp, ch1, join with ss to top of ch3. (15 ch-1 spaces)

Round 4: Ch3 (counts as 1tr/1dc), [1tr/1dc, ch1 (counts as corner), 2tr/2dc] into ch-1 sp at base of ch3, *[ch1, 2tr/2dc in next ch-1 sp] twice, ch1, [2tr/2dc, ch1 (counts as corner), 2tr/2dc] into next ch-1 sp; rep from * three times more, [ch1, 2tr/2dc into next ch-1 sp] twice, ch1, join with ss to top of ch3. Fasten off. (20 ch-1 spaces)

Finishing

Weave in any loose ends. Divide pentagons into two groups. Arrange them so that one is at the centre and the others are joined to each of the five sides of the centre motif. Join pieces using a slip stitch through the back loops of the chain. Repeat for the second side. Place both pieces right sides together and join with slip stitch again, leaving an opening large enough to turn the shape inside out. Cut the legs off an old pair of tights and start to fill with toy stuffing. Place inside the toy and push stuffing down into the corners. When the toy is sufficiently stuffed, tie off the tights and cut off any waste, then close the hole with slip stitch as before.

This soft and interesting toy is a modern take on the traditional baby ball. Try adding extra interest by including a small bell when you stuff the piece. This project is also a great way of using up lots of odds and ends of yarn and a chance to practise the slip-stitch method of joining shapes together.

Little book of shapes

Baby's first book in colourful crochet

Materials

One 50g (115m/126yd) ball of Rowan Cotton Glacé (or equivalent yarn: 4ply/sport-weight 100% mercerized cotton) in each of:

Green (A)
Purple (B)
Red (C)
Sky blue (D)
Orange (E)
3.00mm (US: C-2/D-3) and 3.50mm (US: E-4) hooks
Stitch markers

Size

Outer covers approx. 15cm (6in) square; inner pages approx. 12.5cm (5in) square

Tension (Gauge)

23 sts and 27 rows to 10cm (4in) using 3.50mm (US: E-4) hook and measured over double crochet (US: single crochet).

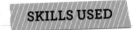

SKILLS USED

· Crocheting varied shapes
· Joining crocheted pieces together
· Making crochet motifs

Front & Back cover (both alike)

Foundation ring: Using 3.00mm (C-2/D-3) hook and yarn A, ch8 and join with a ss to form a ring.

Round 1: Ch3 (counts as 1tr/1dc), 15tr/15dc into the ring, join with ss to 3rd of 3ch and changing to yarn B.

Round 2: Ch5 (counts as 1tr/1dc and 2ch), [1tr/1dc into next tr/dc, 2ch] fifteen times, join with ss to 3rd of 3ch. Break yarn B.

Round 3: Join yarn C to any ch-2 sp, ch3 (counts as 1tr/1dc), 2tr/2dc into same space, 1ch, *[3tr/3dc, 1ch] into next ch-2 sp; rep from * to end of round and join with ss to 3rd of 3ch. Break yarn C.

Front and back cover

ss to 3rd of 3ch. Break yarn D.

Round 6: Join yarn E to any tr/dc along one side of the square, ch3, work 1tr/1dc into each tr/dc of previous round, working [1tr/1dc, 1dtr/1tr, 1tr/1dc] into each ch-2 corner sp, join with ss to 3rd of 3ch and changing to yarn A.

Round 7: Ch3, 1tr/1dc into every tr/dc of previous round, working [1tr/1dc, 1ch, 1dtr/1tr, 1ch, 1tr/1dc] into each dtr/tr at corner, join with ss to 3rd of 3ch and changing to yarn B.

Round 8: Ch3, 1tr/1dc into every tr/dc of previous round, working [1tr/1dc, 1dtr/1tr, 1tr/1dc] into each dtr/tr at corner, join with ss to 3rd of 3ch. Fasten off.

Pages (make 4)

Make one page in each of yarns A, B, D and E.

Using 3.50mm (E-4) hook, make 31 ch.

Row 1: 1dc/1sc into second ch from hook, 1dc/1sc in every rem ch to end of row, turn.

Row 2: Ch1, 1dc/1sc in every dc/sc to end of row, turn.

Repeat row 2 until work is square. Fasten off.

Round 4: Join yarn D to any ch-1 sp, *[3ch, 1dc/1sc into next ch-1 sp] three times, 6ch to make a corner sp, 1dc/1sc into next ch-1 sp; rep from * to end of round, join with a ss to 3rd of 3ch.

Round 5: Ch3 (counts as 1tr/1dc), 2tr/2dc into first ch-3 sp, 3tr/3dc into each of next two ch-3 sps, *[5tr/5dc, 2ch, 5tr/5dc] into 6ch corner sp, 3tr/3dc into each ch-3 sp; rep from * to end of round, join with a

Pages

Square and circle

Shapes

SQUARE

Using 3.00mm (C-2/D-3) hook and yarn B, ch4 and join with a ss to form a ring.

Round 1: Ch5 (counts as 1tr/1dc and 2ch), [3tr/3dc into ring, ch2] three times, 2tr/2dc into ring, join with a ss to 3rd of 5ch.

Round 2: Ss into the next ch sp, ch7, (counts as 1tr/1dc and ch4), 2tr/2dc into the sp at the base of the ch, *1tr/1dc in each of the next 3tr/3dc, [2tr/2dc, ch4, 2tr/2dc] in the next sp; rep from * twice more, 1tr/1dc in each of the next 3tr/3dc, 1tr/1dc in the same sp as ch7, join with ss to 3rd of 7ch.

Round 3: Ss into the next ch sp, ch7, (counts as 1tr/1dc and ch4), 2tr/2dc into the sp at the base of the ch, *1tr/1dc in each of the next 7tr/7dc, [2tr/2dc, ch4, 2tr/2dc] in the next sp; rep from * twice more, 1tr/1dc in each of the next 7tr/7dc, 1tr/1dc in the same sp as ch7, join with ss to 3rd of 7ch. Fasten off.

CIRCLE

Using 3.00mm (C-2/D-3) hook and yarn C, ch 6 and join with a ss to form a ring.

Round 1: Ch5 (counts as 1tr/1dc, 2ch), [1tr/1dc, ch2] into ring seven times, join with a ss to 3rd of 5ch. 8 spaced tr/8 spaced dc

Round 2: Ch3 (counts as 1tr/1dc), 2tr/2dc into same place, ch2, [3tr/3dc into next tr/dc, ch2] seven times, join with a ss into 3rd of 3ch.

Round 3: Ch3 (counts as 1tr/1dc), 1tr/1dc into same place, 1tr/1dc into next tr/dc, 2tr/2dc into next tr/dc, ch2, [2tr/2dc into next tr/dc, 1tr/1dc into next tr/dc, 2tr/2dc into next tr/dc, ch2] seven times, join with a ss into 3rd of 3ch. Fasten off.

TRIANGLE

Using 3.00mm (C-2/D-3) hook and yarn E, ch 8 and join with a ss to form a ring.

Round 1: Ch3 (counts as 1tr/1dc), 2tr/2dc into ring, ch3, [3tr/3dc, ch3] twice, join with a ss to 3rd of 3ch. (You will have 9tr/9dc and 3 ch-3 sp.)

Round 2: Ch3 (counts as 1tr/1dc), 1tr/1dc into each of next 2 sts, *[3tr/3dc, ch3, 3tr/3dc] into next ch-3 sp, 1tr/1dc in each of next 3 sts; rep from * once more, [3tr/3dc, ch3, 3tr/3dc] into next ch-3 sp, join with a ss to 3rd of 3ch. (You will have 27tr/27dc and 3 ch-3 sp.)

Round 3: Ch3 (counts as 1tr/1dc), 1tr/1dc

Triangle and diamond

D, ch4 and join with a ss to form a ring.

Round 1: Ch1, [1dc/1sc, 1htr/1hdc, 1tr/1dc, 1dtr/1tr, ch3, 1dtr/1tr, 1tr/1dc, 1htr/1hdc] twice into the ring, join with a ss to 1ch.

Round 2: Ch5 (counts as 1tr/1dc and ch2), 1tr/1dc in dc/sc, 1tr/1dc in each of next 3 sts [3tr/3dc, ch4, 3tr/3dc] into ch-3 sp, 1tr/1dc in each of next 3 sts, 1tr/1dc, ch2, 1tr/1dc in next dc/sc, 1tr/1dc in each of next 3 sts [3tr/3dc, ch4, 3tr/3dc] into ch-3 sp, 1tr/1dc in each of next 3 sts, join with ss in 3rd of beg 5ch.

Round 3: Ch3 (counts as 1tr/1dc), *[1tr/1dc, ch3, 1tr/1dc] into next ch-2 sp, 1tr/1dc in next 2tr/2dc, ch1, miss next tr/dc, 1tr/1dc in each of next 3tr/3dc, ch1, miss next tr/dc, [3tr/3dc, ch5, 3tr/3dc] into next ch-4 sp, ch1, miss next tr/dc, 1tr/1dc in each of next 3tr/3dc, ch1, miss next tr/dc, 1tr/1dc in each of next 2tr/2dc; rep from * once more, miss the last tr/dc at the end of the last rep, join with a ss to 3rd of 3ch. Fasten off.

into each of next 5 sts, *[3tr/3dc, ch3, 3tr/3dc] into next ch-3 sp, 1tr/1dc in each of next 9 sts; rep from * once more, [3tr/3dc, ch3, 3tr/3dc] into next ch-3 sp, 1tr/1dc in each of next 3 sts, join with a ss to 3rd of 3ch. (You will have 45tr/45dc and 3 ch-3 sp.) Fasten off.

DIAMOND

Using 3.00mm (C-2/D-3) hook and yarn

HEXAGON

Using 3.00mm (C-2/D-3) hook and yarn A, ch6 and join with a ss to form a ring.

Hexagon and heart

Round 1: Ch6 (counts as 1dtr/1tr and ch2), [1dtr/1tr into ring, ch2] eleven times, join with a ss to 4th of 6ch. (You will have 12 ch-2 sp).

Round 2: Ss in next ch-2 sp, ch3 (counts as 1tr/1dc), [1tr/1dc, ch2, 2tr/2dc] into the ch-2 sp at the base of the beg ch3, [1tr/1dc into next ch-2 sp, (2tr/2dc, ch2, 2tr/2dc) into next ch-2 sp] five times, 3tr/3dc into next ch-2 sp, join with a ss to 3rd of 3ch.

Round 3: Ch1, 1dc/1sc into each of next 2tr/2dc, [(2dc/2sc, ch1, 2dc/2sc) into the ch-2 sp, 1dc/1sc into each of next 7tr/7dc] five times, (2dc/2sc, ch1, 2dc/2sc) into next ch-2 sp, 1dc/1sc into each of next 5tr/5dc, join with a ss to 1ch. Fasten off.

HEART

Using 3.00mm (C-2/D-3) hook and yarn B, ch17.

Round 1: 3htr/3hdc into 2nd ch from hook, 1htr/1hdc into each of next 6ch, miss next 2ch, 1htr/1hdc in each of next 6ch, 3htr/3hdc in next ch, continue by working into each chain loop on opposite side of the foundation ch, 1htr/1hdc in next 6ch, [1htr/1hdc, ch2, 1htr/1hdc] into next ch-2 sp, 1htr/1hdc in each of last 6ch, DO NOT JOIN. (32 sts)

Round 2: 2htr/2hdc in each of next 3 sts, 1htr/1hdc in each of next 5 sts, miss next 2 sts, 1htr/1hdc in each of next 5 sts, 2htr/2hdc in each of the next 3 sts, 1htr/1hdc in each of the next 7 sts, [1htr/1hdc, ch2, 1htr/1hdc] into next ch-2 sp, 1htr/1hdc in each of last 7 sts. (38 sts)

Round 3: [2htr/2hdc in next st, 1htr/1hdc in next st] three times, 1htr/1hdc in each of next 4 sts, miss next 2 sts, 1htr/1hdc in each of next 4 sts, [2htr/2hdc in next st, 1htr/1hdc in next st] three times, 1htr/1hdc in each of next 8 sts, [1htr/1hdc, ch2, 1htr/1hdc] into next ch-2 sp, 1htr/1hdc in each of last 8 sts. (44 sts)

Round 4: 1htr/1hdc in next st, [2htr/2hdc in next st, 1htr/1hdc in each of next 2 sts] three times, 1htr/1hdc in each of next 2 sts, miss next 2 sts, 1htr/1hdc in each of next 4 sts, [2htr/2hdc in next st, 1htr/1hdc in each of next 2 sts] three times, 1htr/1hdc in each of next 8 sts, [1htr/1hdc, ch2, 1htr/1hdc] into next ch-2 sp, 1htr/1hdc in each of last 8 sts. (50 sts) Fasten off.

Not only is this little book fun to crochet, but it makes an ideal gift for a newborn. The bright colours and shapes will appeal to the very young and the book is easily held by little fingers. This piece will also give you a chance to explore how different shapes are constructed.

Finishing

Weave in any loose ends and press lightly according to ball band instructions. Arrange pages in the following order: A, B, E and D. Leave the front of the first page blank and then slipstitch the square to the back of page 1 (worked in A), the circle to the front and triangle to the back of page 2 (worked in B), the diamond to the front of and the hexagon to the back of page 3 (worked in E) and, finally, the heart to the front of page 4 (worked in D).

When pages are complete, arrange in the correct order. Using 3.50mm (E-4) hook and yarn B, join yarn through all 4 pages at top left-hand corner with ss.
Row 1: Ch1, work 1dc/1sc into same place, work 1dc/1sc into row ends until you reach the bottom of the pages. (16 dc/16 sc)
Fasten off.
This creates the spine.
Place markers either side of the centre 16 sts of the front and back covers of the book. Join yarn B to top left-hand corners with a ss.
Row 1: Ch1, work 1dc/1sc into next st of both pieces of fabric until you reach the marker, insert pages, remove marker and then continue to work 1dc/1sc through front cover, dc/sc on 'spine' of pages and back cover, until you reach the second marker, remove and then continue as before until you reach the last st, turn.
Row 2: Ch1, 1dc/1sc in every dc/sc to end of row. Fasten off.
Weave in any further loose ends.

Peaceful baby blanket

Beautiful blanket worked in soft shell stitches

Materials
Rowan Cashsoft 4 Ply (160m/175yd per 50g ball; or equivalent yarn: 4ply/sportweight cashmere, merino and acrylic blend):
Four balls in cream (A)
Three balls in dark beige (B)
Three balls in green (C)
One ball in pale blue (D)
3.00mm (US: C-2/D-3) hook

Size
Approx. 66 x 84 cm (26 x 33in)

Tension (Gauge)
16 sts and 12 rows to 10cm (4in) using 3.00mm (US: C-2/D-3) hook and measured over pattern.

Special abbreviations
Tr5tog (US: dc5tog) = treble (US: double crochet) the next 5 stitches together

Pattern note
Stripe sequence (over 12 rows):

Row 1: B.
Row 2 and every foll alt RS row: A.
Row 3: C.
Row 5: B.
Row 7: C.
Row 9: B.
Row 11: D.
Row 12: As row 2.

Blanket
Using 3.00mm (C-2/D-3) hook and yarn A, ch 153.
Foundation row (RS): Miss first 2ch (counts as 1tr/1dc), 2tr/2dc into next ch, miss 2ch, 1dc/1sc into next ch, *miss 2ch, 5tr/5dc into next ch, miss 2ch, 1dc/1sc in

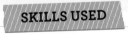

SKILLS USED

- Making shell stitches with decreases
- Changing colours
- Working a neat edging